Overwatch

The Ultimate Book of Memes

Introduction

Congratulations on purchasing your own copy of Overwatch Memes. I hope you LOVE these memes!

Included are over 100 of the funniest memes related to Overwatch, we hope you get as much enjoyment out of them as we did!

Team: We need a healer
Hanzo:

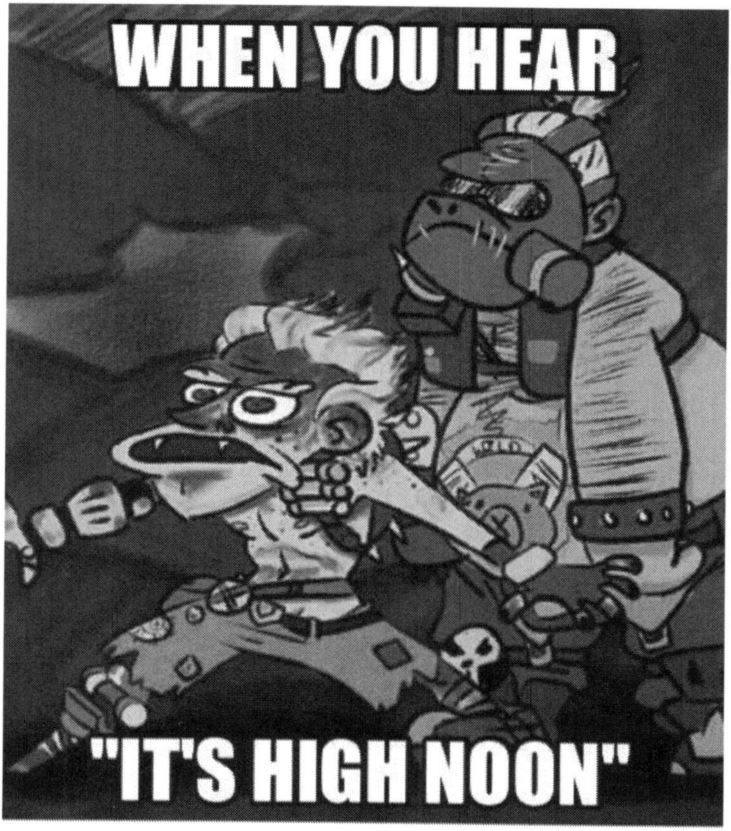
WHEN YOU HEAR
"IT'S HIGH NOON"

Me: Hears Gabriel's voice before he turned into Reaper

Me:

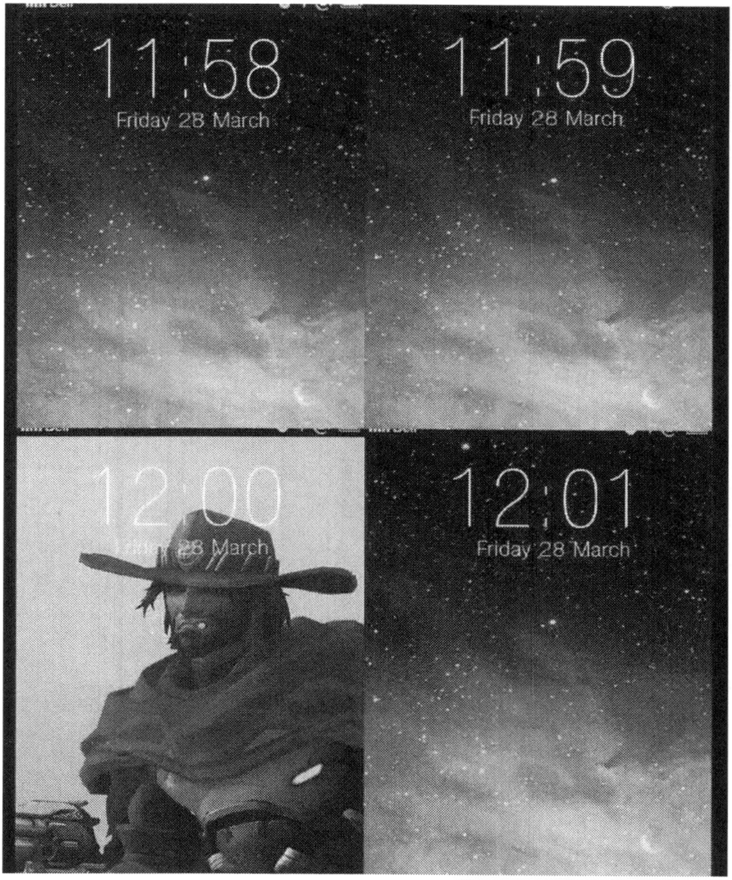
11:58
Friday 28 March
11:59
Friday 28 March
12:00
28 March
12:01
Friday 28 March

be careful who you call ugly in middle school

when no one on ur team watches for flankers and trickle into death

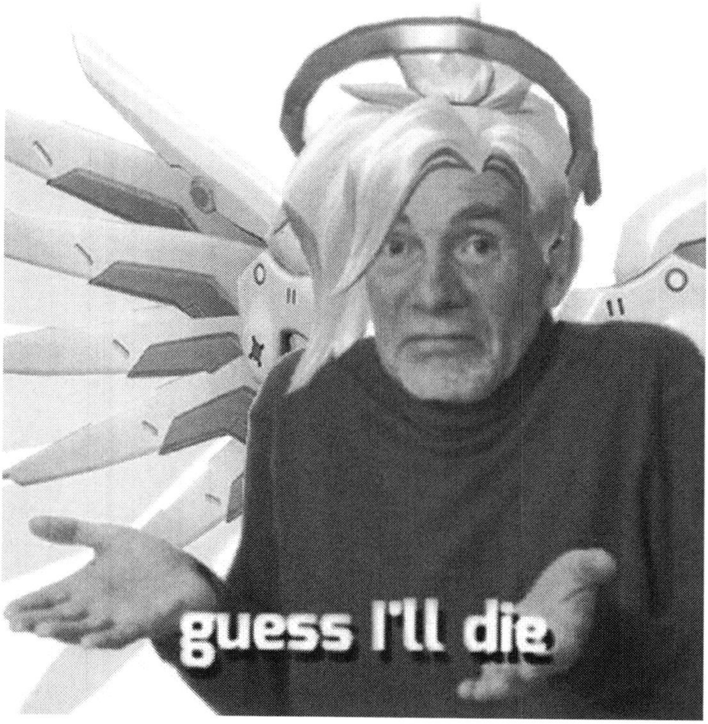
guess I'll die.

LÚCIO
VOICE LINES
YOU GOTTA BELIEVE!
BE CHAMPIONS
4025
BOOP
EQUIP
BOOP (75)
I am the one who boops!
amc

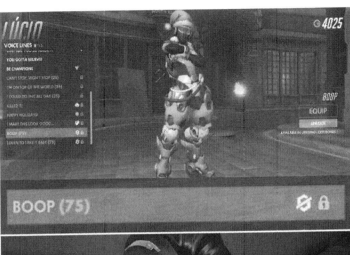

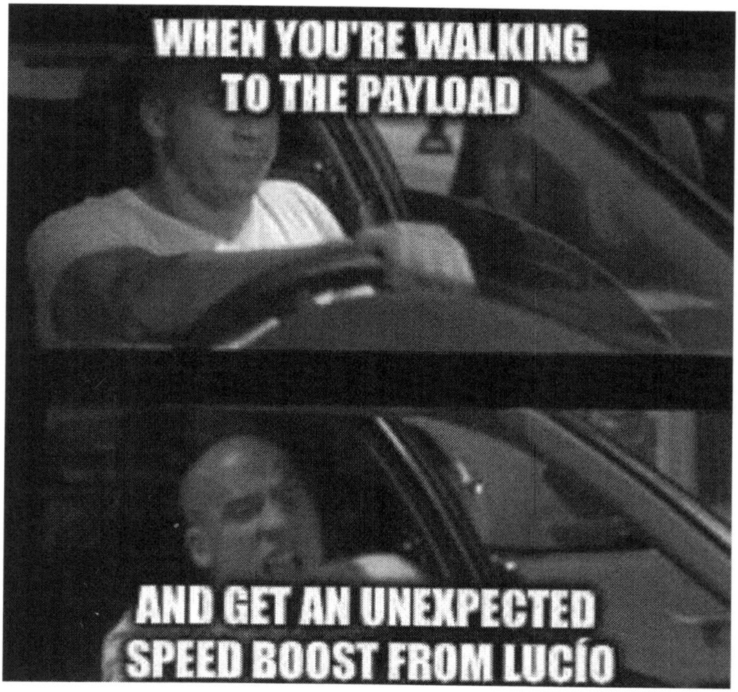
WHEN YOU'RE WALKING
TO THE PAYLOAD
AND GET AN UNEXPECTED
SPEED BOOST FROM LUCÍO

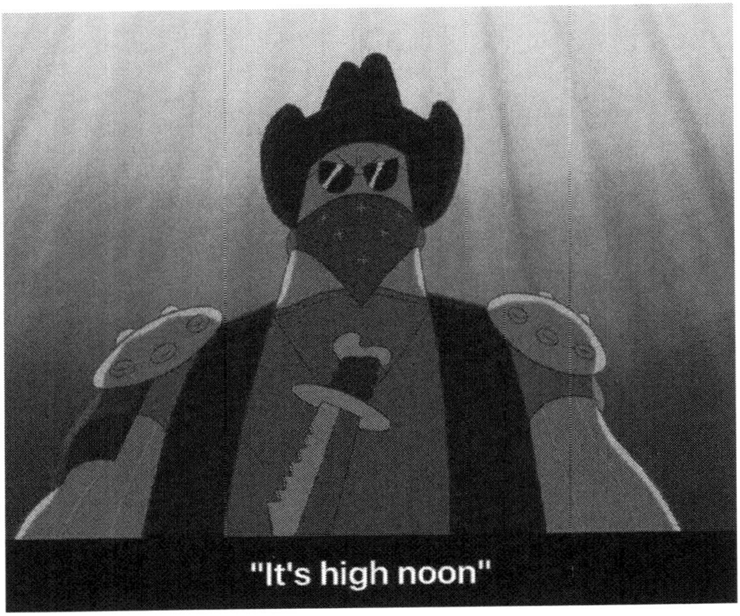
"It's high noon"

That Genji won't need healing if you let him die

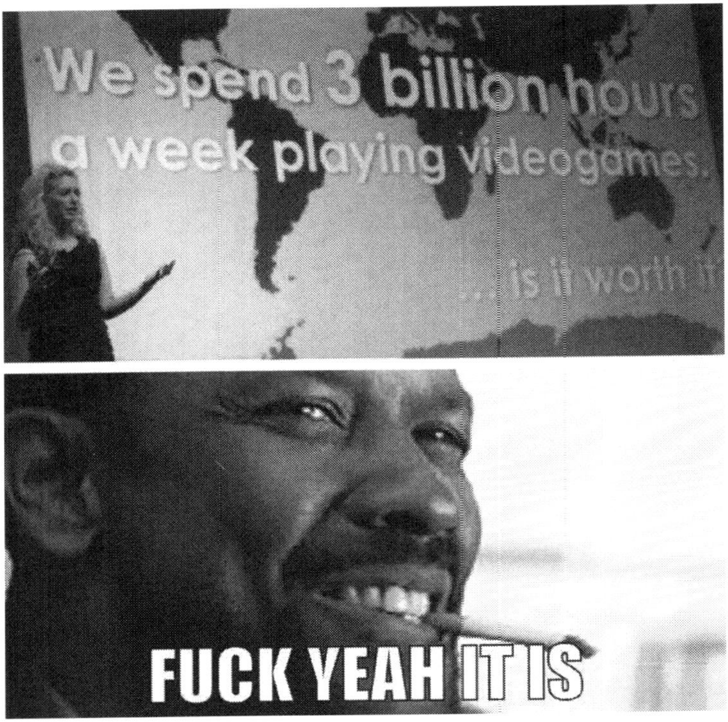
We spend 3 billion hours a week playing videogames.
... is it worth it
FUCK YEAH IT IS

You can't be asked to stay on the payload if you never get near it.

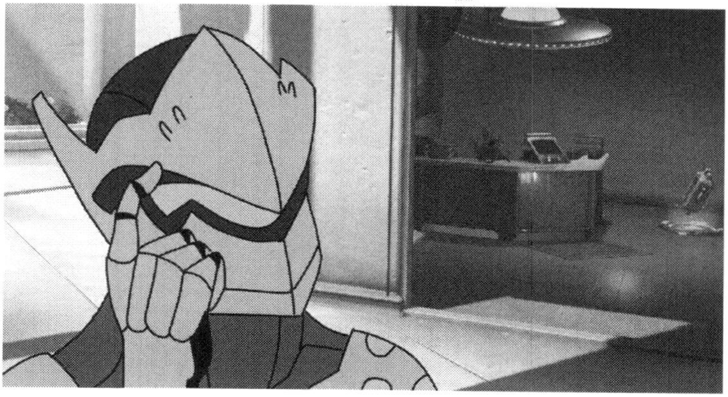

"Twenty years after we won the war against the om-"

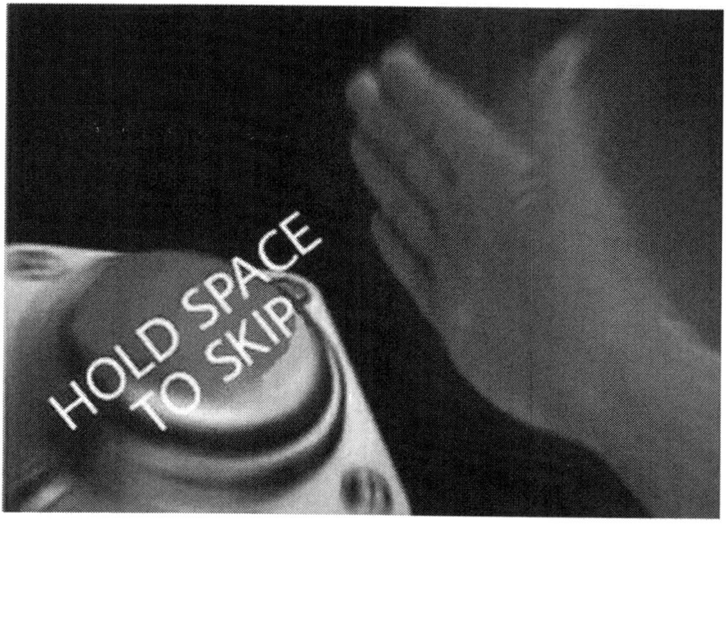
HOLD SPACE
TO SKIP

When you go to bed and lay there recalling all the shit games you just played.

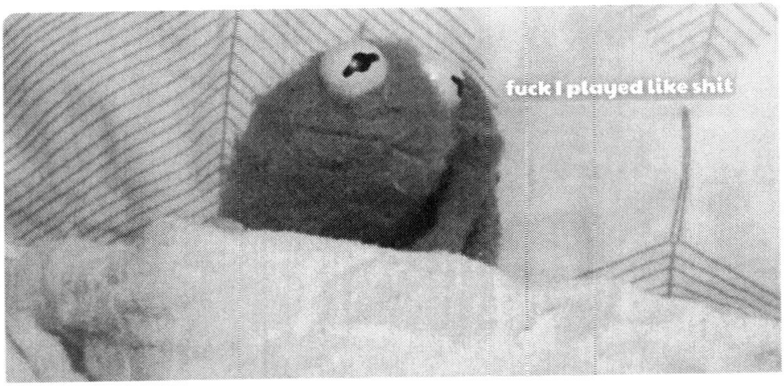
fuck I played like shit

when you rush right in there with a really good
argument but then forget it immediately

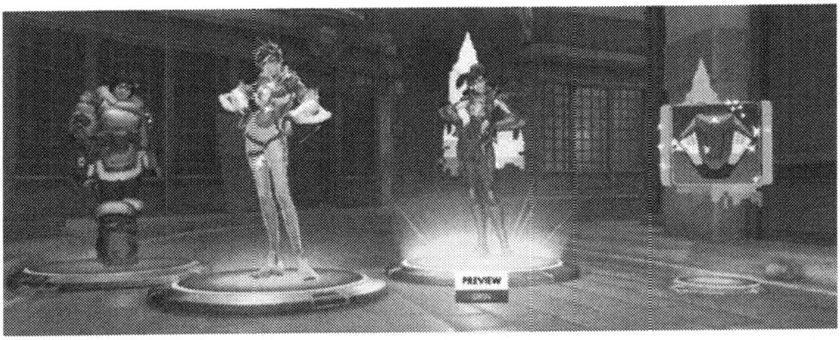
PREVIEW
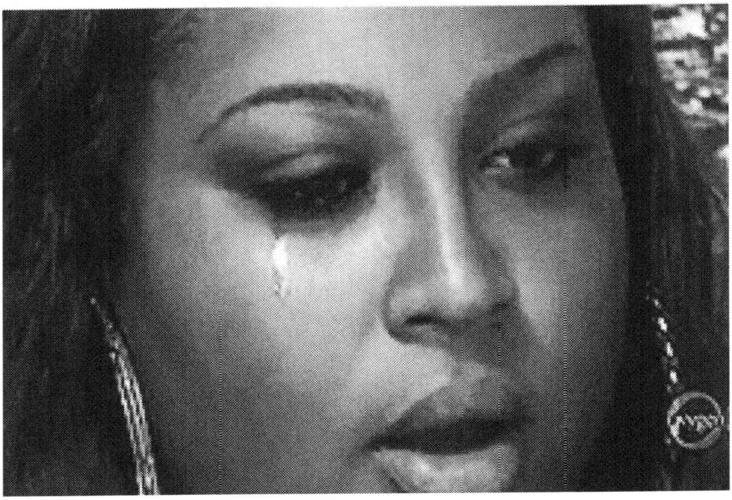

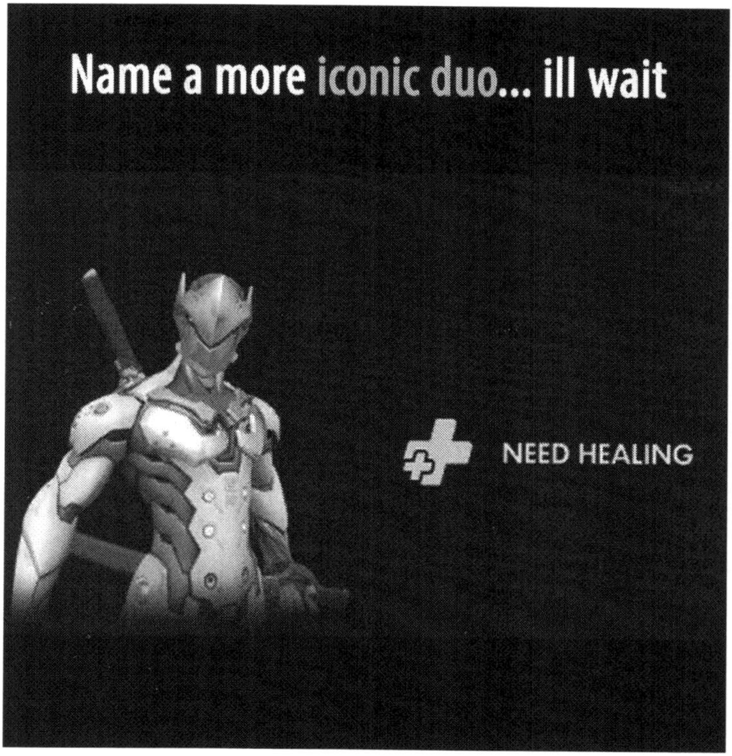
Name a more iconic duo... ill wait
NEED HEALING

When you try to stay positive but your team has 2 snipers and 3 DPS

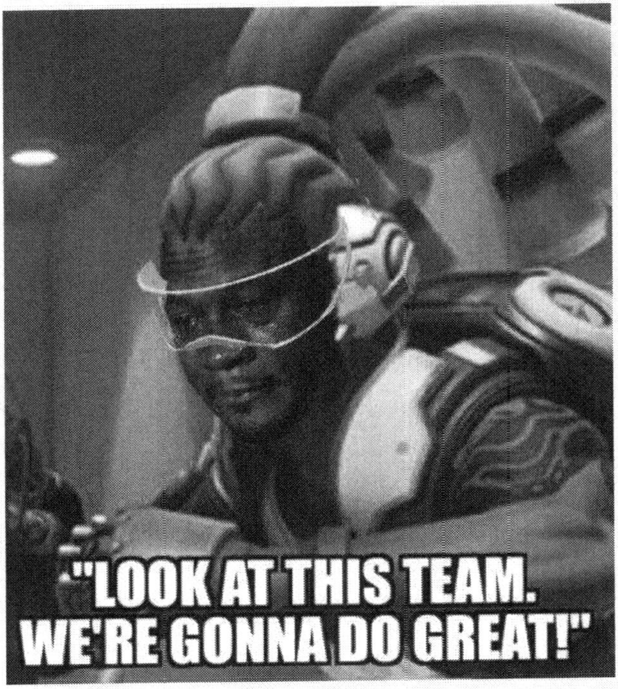
"LOOK AT THIS TEAM.
WE'RE GONNA DO GREAT!"

When you watch the Pharah you just hacked struggle on the ground.

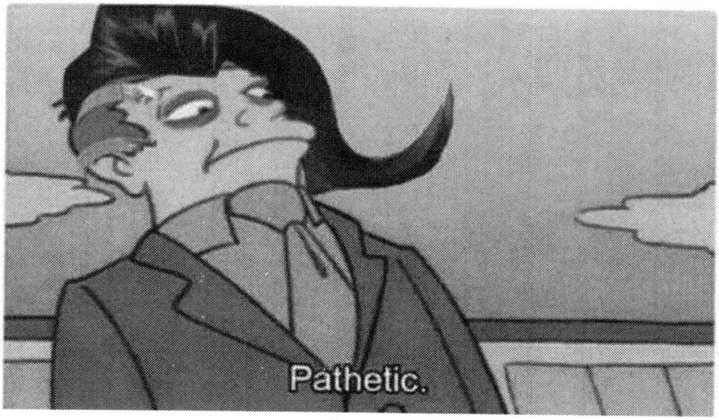
Pathetic.

**When they call you a hacker
but they don't know that you missed
50 shots before hitting them**

When a support player is suddenly expected to play offensive

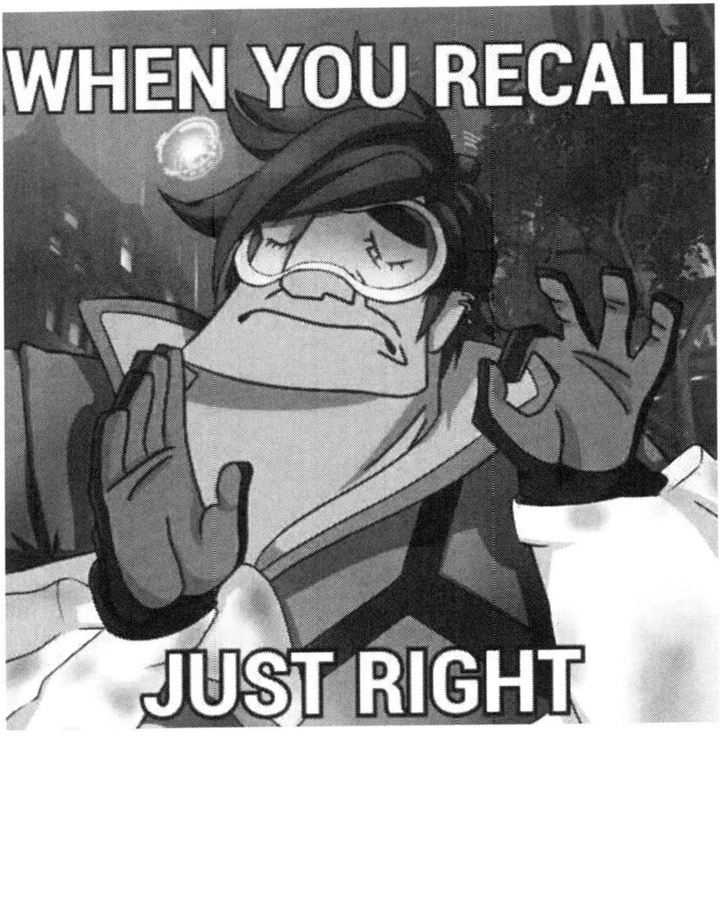
WHEN YOU RECALL
JUST RIGHT

I... I- I
OMG hes about to say his first words
I need healing

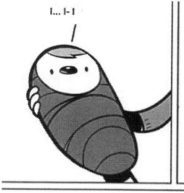

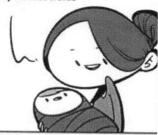

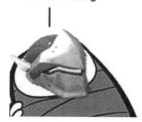

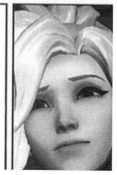

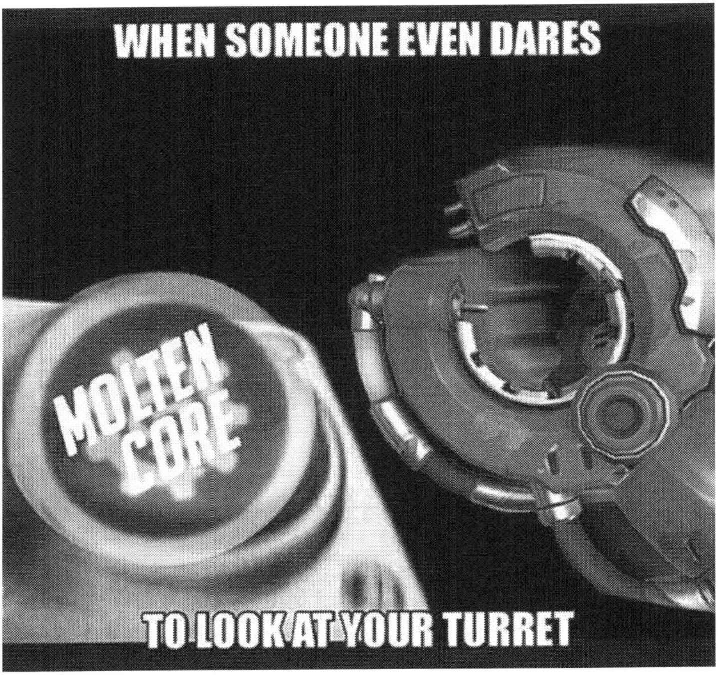
WHEN SOMEONE EVEN DARES
MOLTEN CORE
TO LOOK AT YOUR TURRET

when you capping the point and you hear "NERF THIS"

HOW TO WIN MY HEART :

 X1

 X50

When you're the only one sitting on the payload.

WHEN YOU ONLY NEED 1 MORE WIN TO RANK UP

AND YOU LOSE 6 IN A ROW INSTEAD...

When you hear "it's high noon" but you can't find McCree

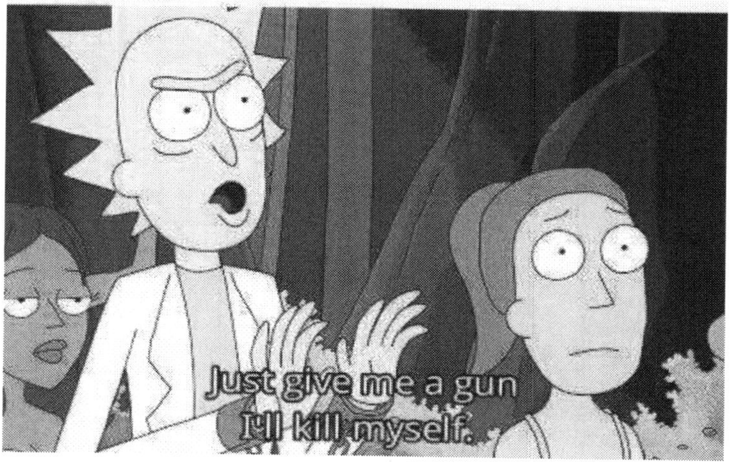
Just give me a gun
I'll kill myself.

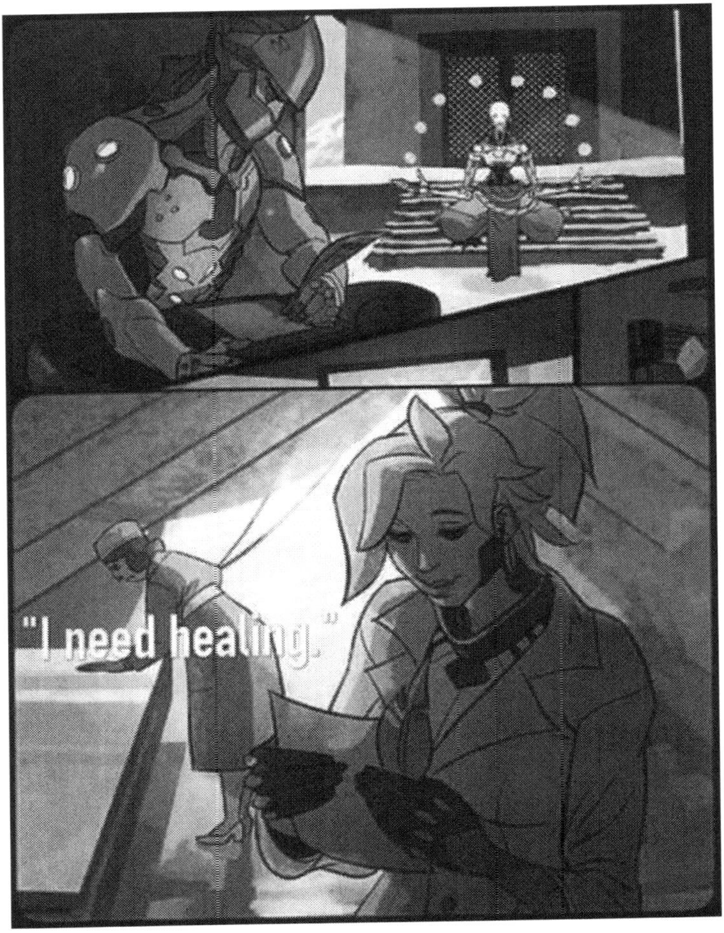
"I need healing."

HOW TO START A CONVERSATION WITH A GIRL:

 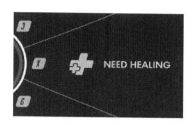

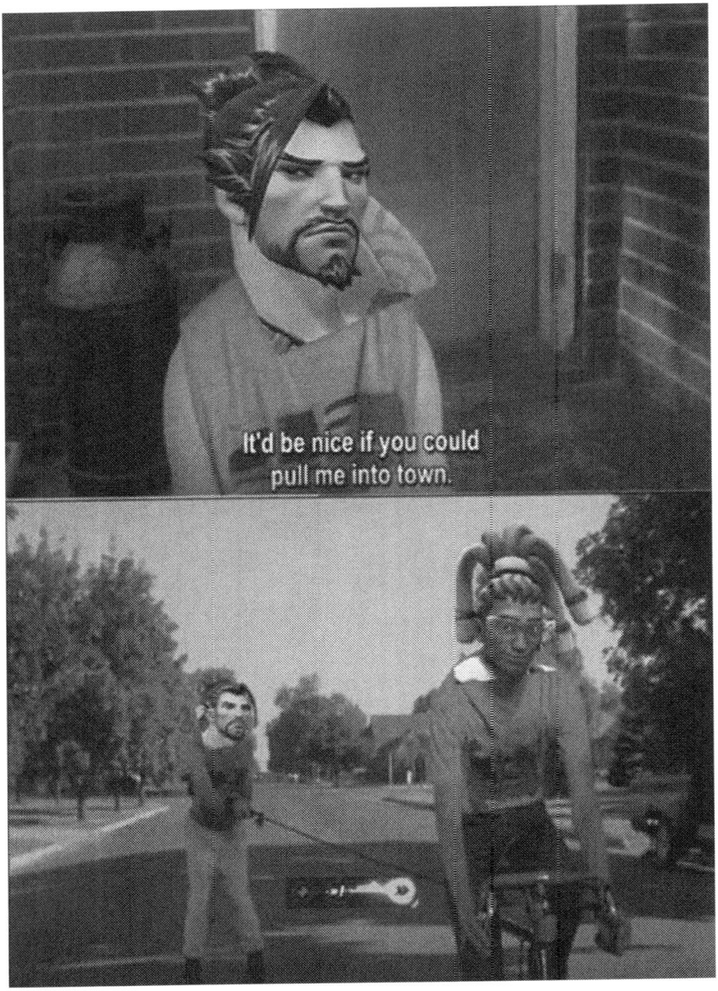
It'd be nice if you could
pull me into town.

When you're a Hanzo and you don't get a headshot after shooting someone in their shoulder

AT&T
10:00 PM
Blizzard Technical Support
00:06
mute
keypad
speaker
add call
FaceTime
contacts

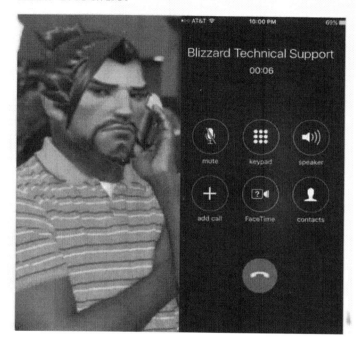

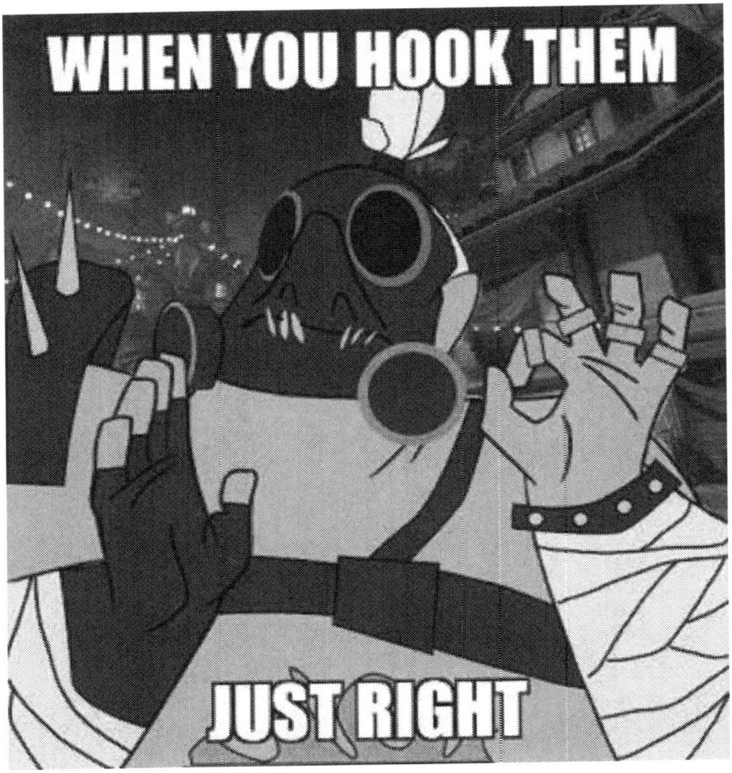
WHEN YOU HOOK THEM
JUST RIGHT

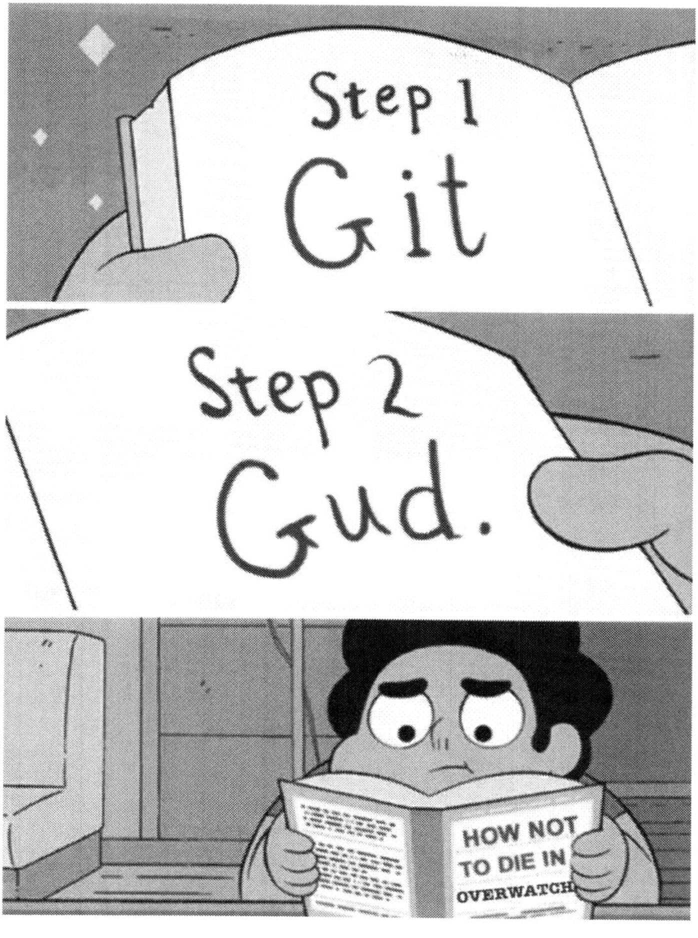
Step 1
Git
Step 2
Gud.
HOW NOT
TO DIE IN
OVERWATCH

Attack commences in 30 secs
#Overwatch

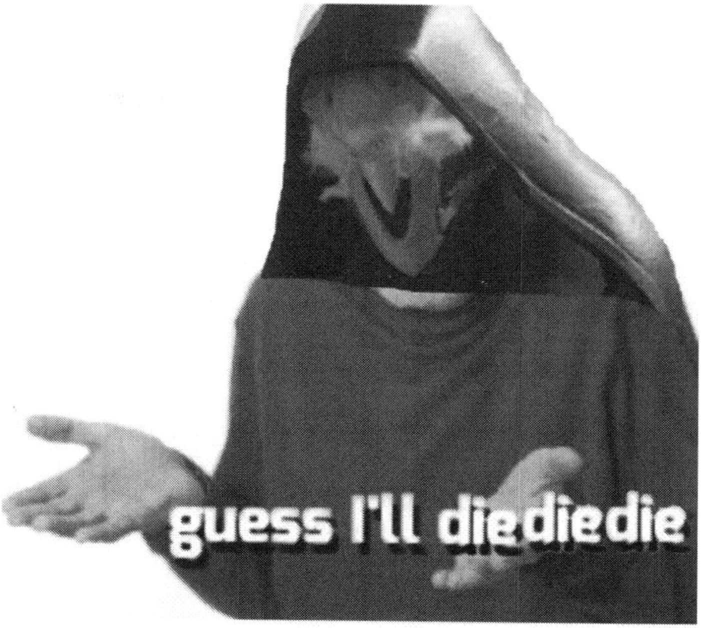
guess I'll diediedie

When you want to save your ult, but you're the only one defending the point

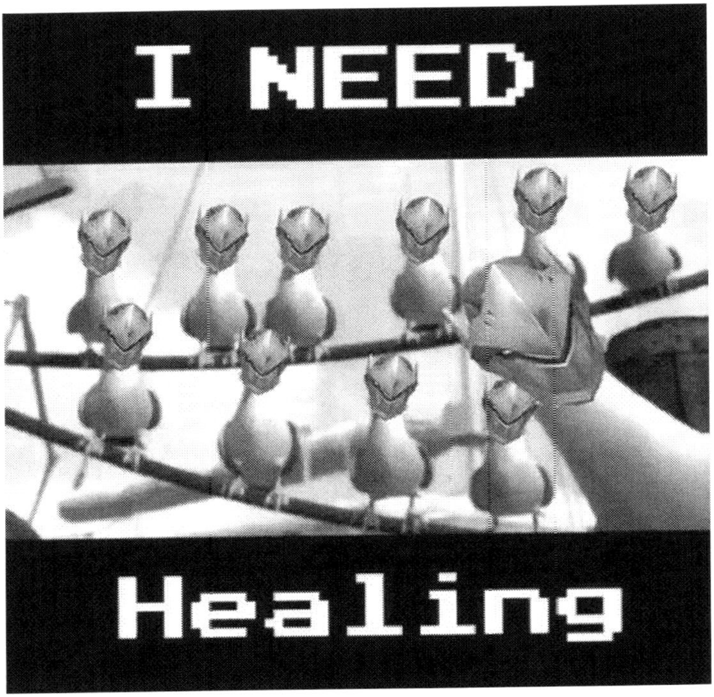
I NEED
Healing

My team: [escorting the payload]

Mcree: It's hiiiiigh noon.

My team:

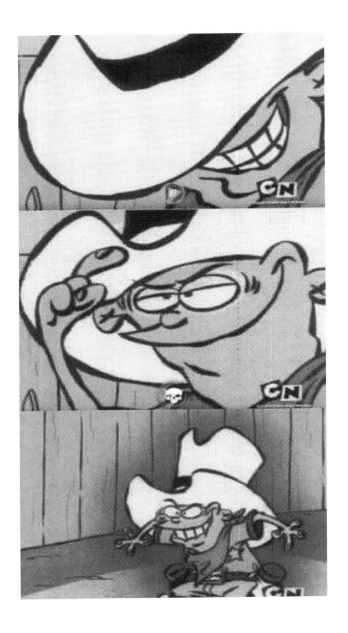

Meeting her parents for the first time vs when you bout to smash

How Lucio came into Overwatch

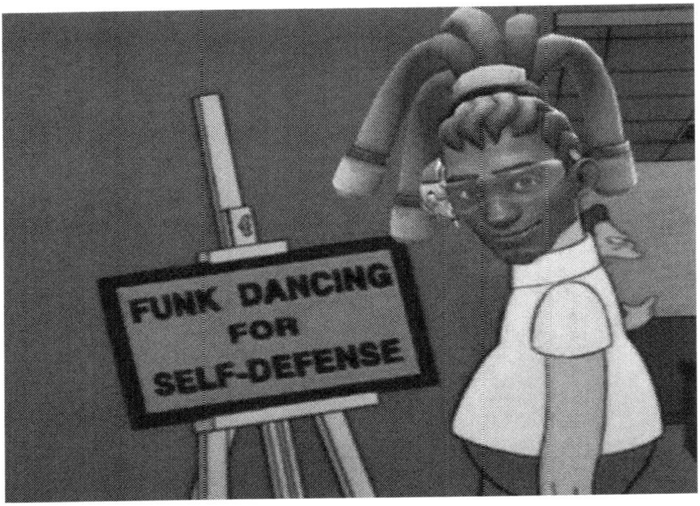
FUNK DANCING
FOR
SELF-DEFENSE

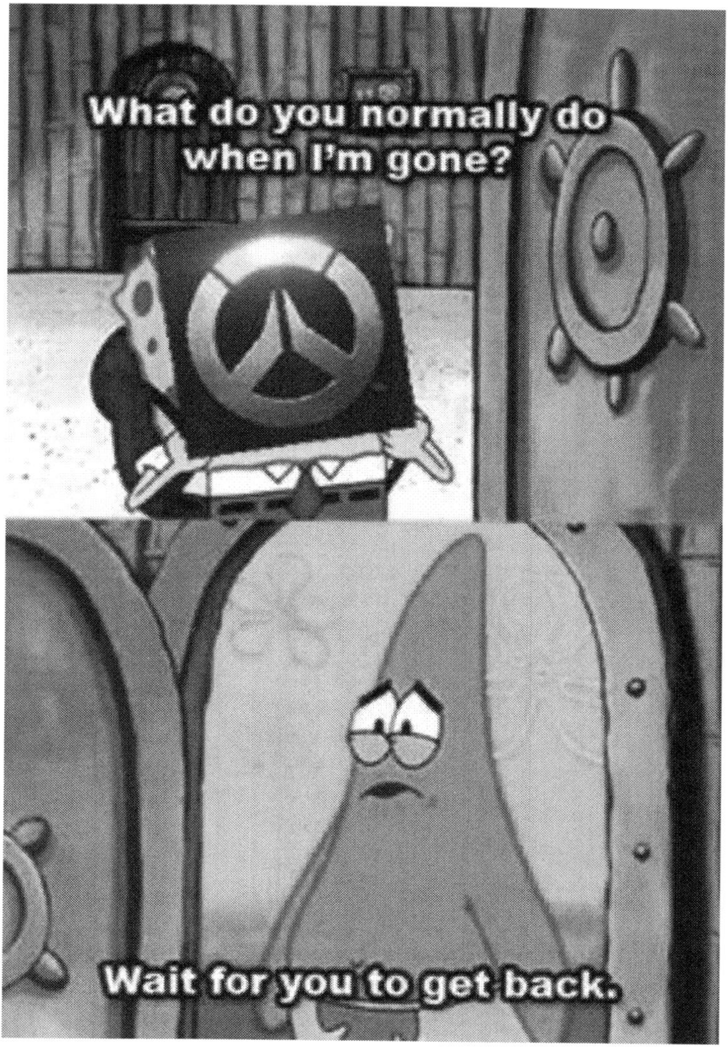
What do you normally do
when I'm gone?
Wait for you to get back.

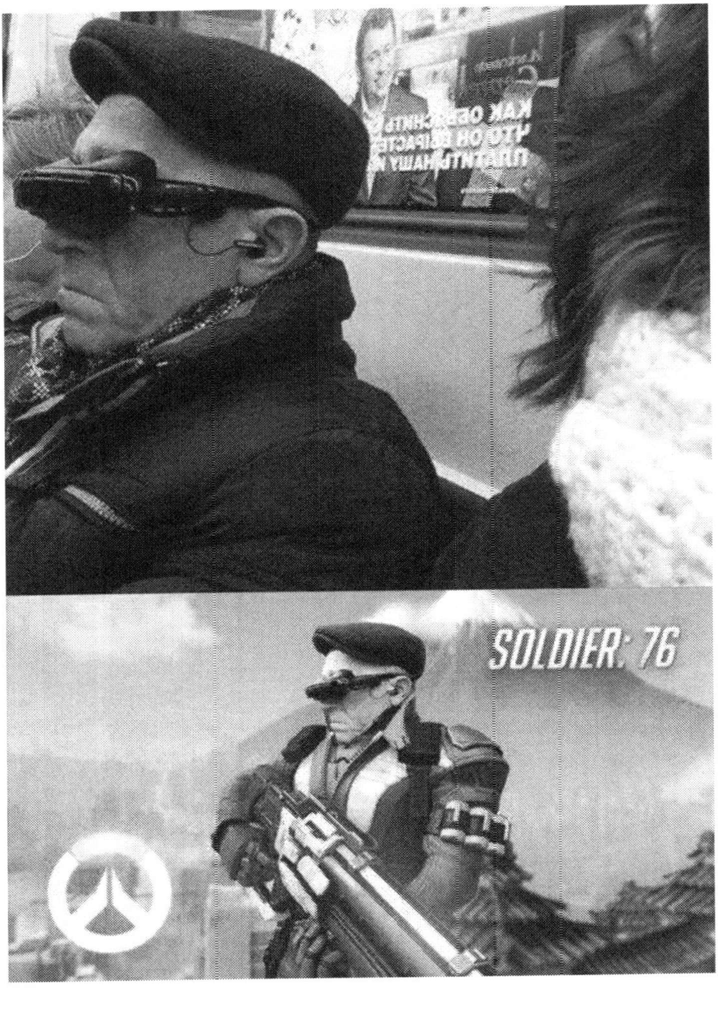
SOLDIER: 76

When my ultimate is ready: "I should really save it for the perfect opportunity"

Me @ me: "or you can use it to kill this Mei"

100% me

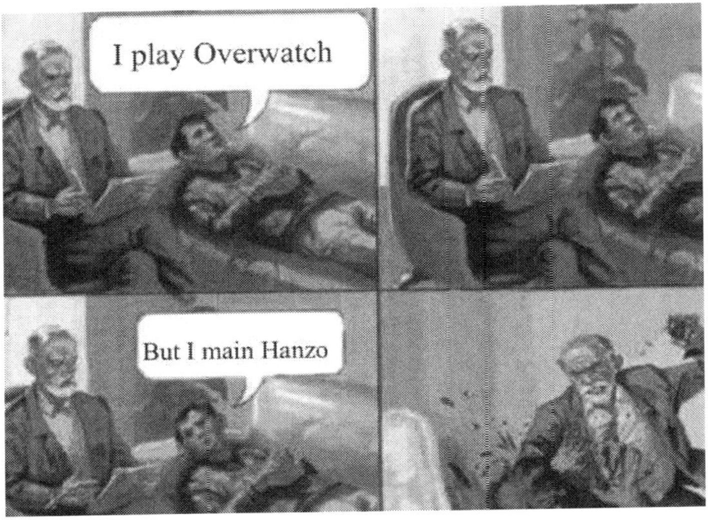
I play Overwatch
But I main Hanzo

When you go to take a bite of your food after getting killed but hear "Heroes never die!"

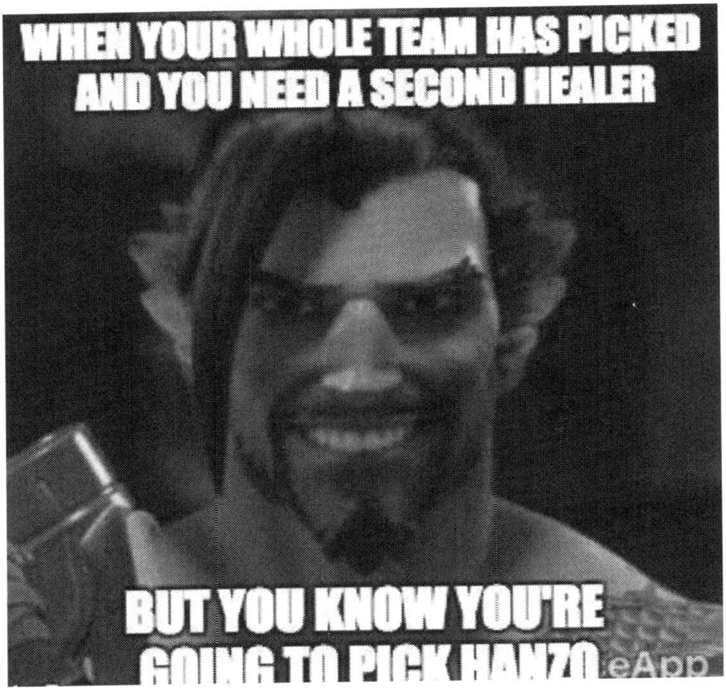
WHEN YOUR WHOLE TEAM HAS PICKED
AND YOU NEED A SECOND HEALER
BUT YOU KNOW YOU'RE
GOING TO PICK HANZO

You can't give the enemy healers ult charge if you never hit anything

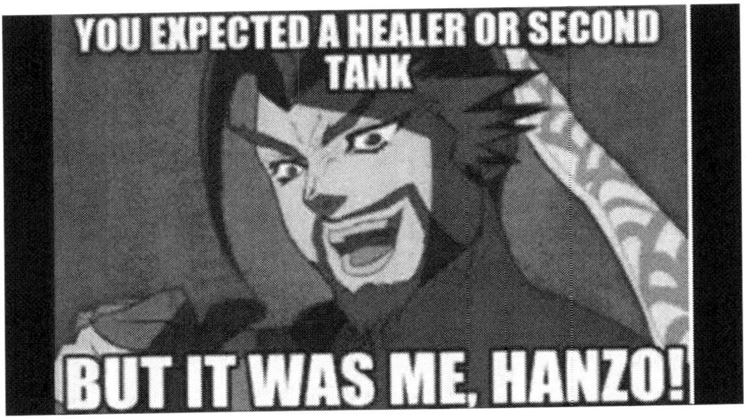
YOU EXPECTED A HEALER OR SECOND TANK
BUT IT WAS ME, HANZO!

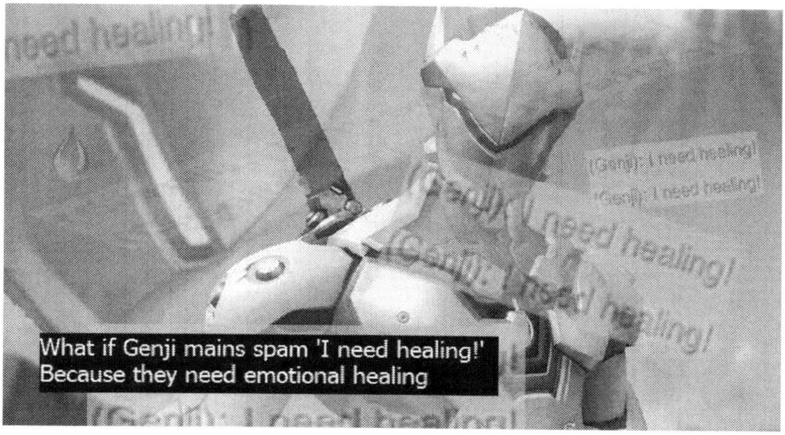
(Genji): I need healing!
(Genji): I need healing!
need healing!
What if Genji mains spam 'I need healing!'
Because they need emotional healing

When Junkrat ults

only to kill you

When Mei freezes you and starts aiming up

Please don't do this.

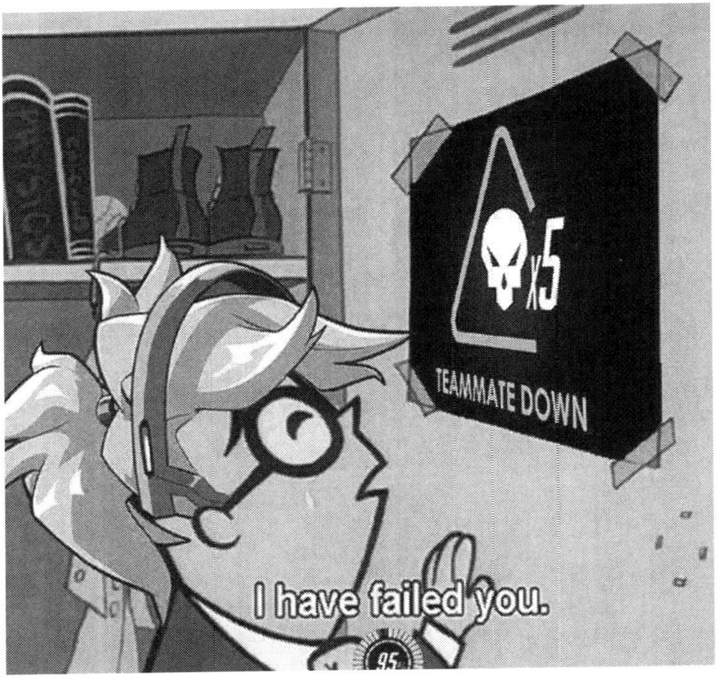
x5
TEAMMATE DOWN
I have failed you.

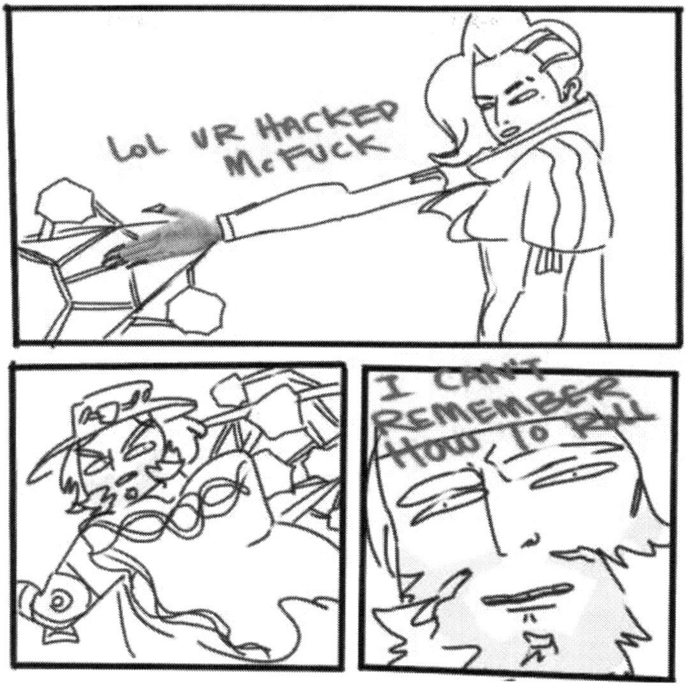
LoL UR HACKED McFUCK
I CAN'T REMEMBER HOW TO

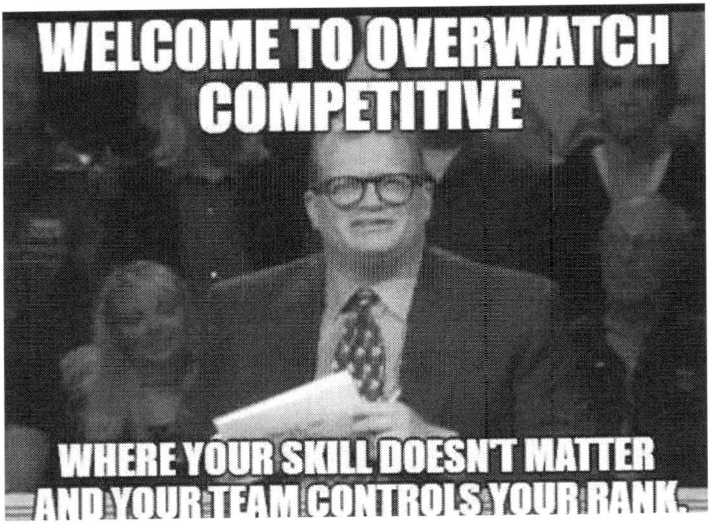
WELCOME TO OVERWATCH
COMPETITIVE
WHERE YOUR SKILL DOESN'T MATTER
AND YOUR TEAM CONTROLS YOUR RANK.

When Mei walls you in with her

Arby's @Arbys · 1h

Our new hire's been killing it

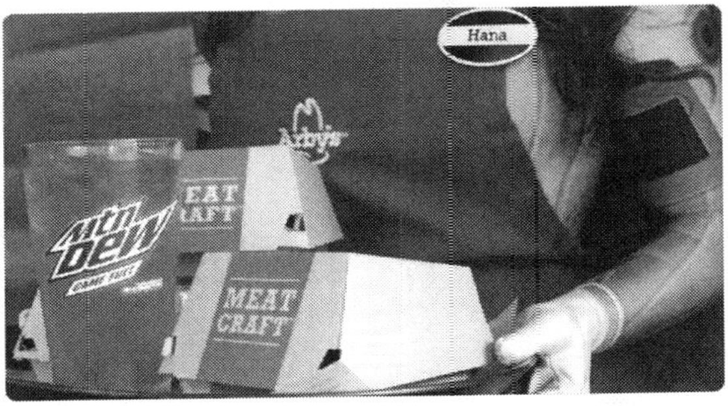
Hana
MEAT
CRAFT

175 2,113 4,332

Blizzard Ent @Blizzard_Ent · 32s

So thaaaats where she's been instead of on the payload 😊✌

2

DAVID HASSELHOFF
GREATEST HITS
incl.
HIT-MIX

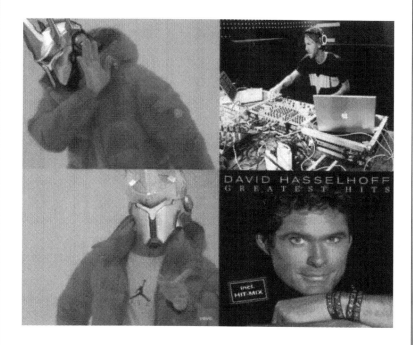

I NEED HEALING!
ill send you my consultation fee
Protect me you dumb fck it costs $0 -mercy

Trust nobody, not even yourself

When that teammate who didn't group up with you says they need healing

its high noon

When your team is mostly tanks but you gotta get 'em to the point first

A boy who knows how to manage their money for the important things in life 👌👌😍

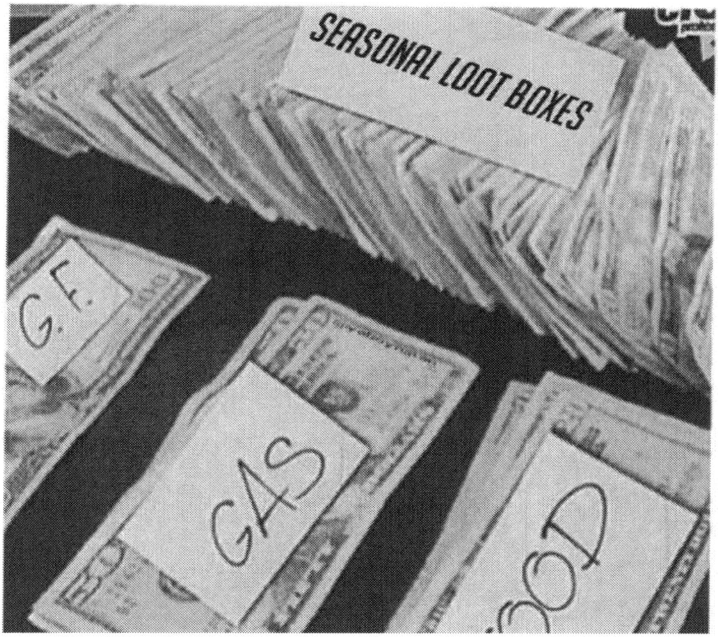
SEASONAL LOOT BOXES
G.F.
GAS

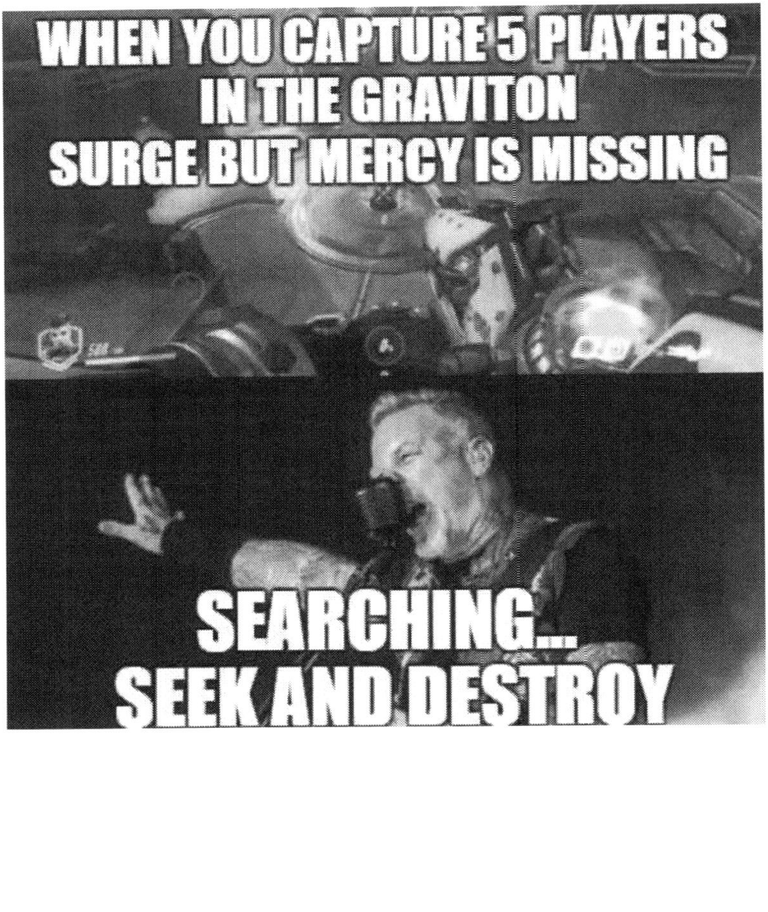
WHEN YOU CAPTURE 5 PLAYERS
IN THE GRAVITON
SURGE BUT MERCY IS MISSING
SEARCHING...
SEEK AND DESTROY

When your man leaves his phone in
the room

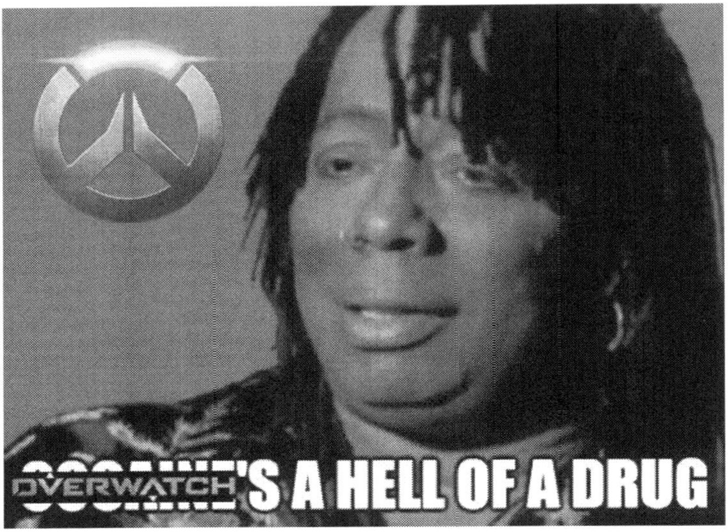
OVERWATCH'S A HELL OF A DRUG

When you ask your team where the enemy Mei is

Speak of the devil

and she shall appear

push the payload
WHOA, THIS LOOKS HARD

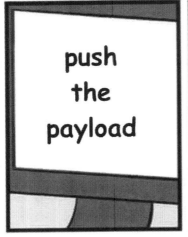

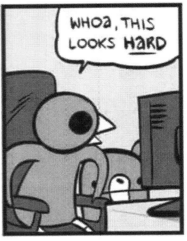

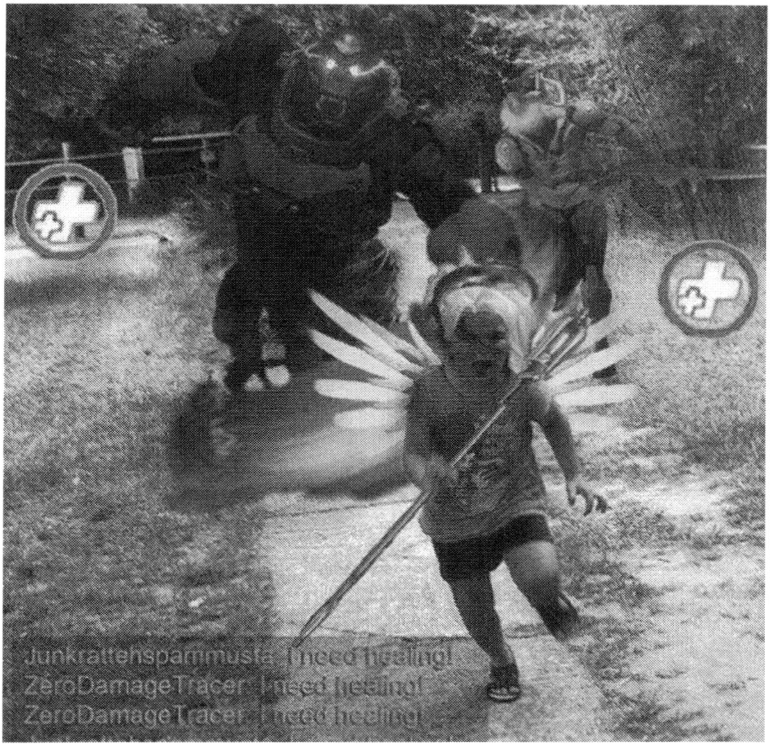
Junkrattehspammusta: I need healing!
ZeroDamageTracer: I need healing!
ZeroDamageTracer: I need healing!

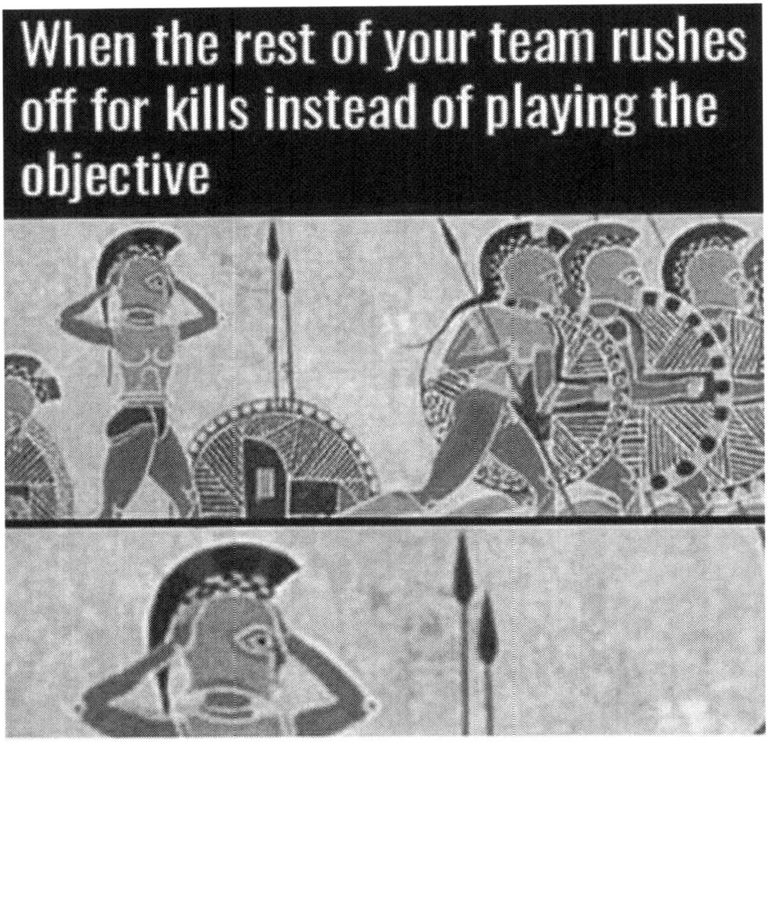
When the rest of your team rushes off for kills instead of playing the objective

Being the first person on your team to select a hero

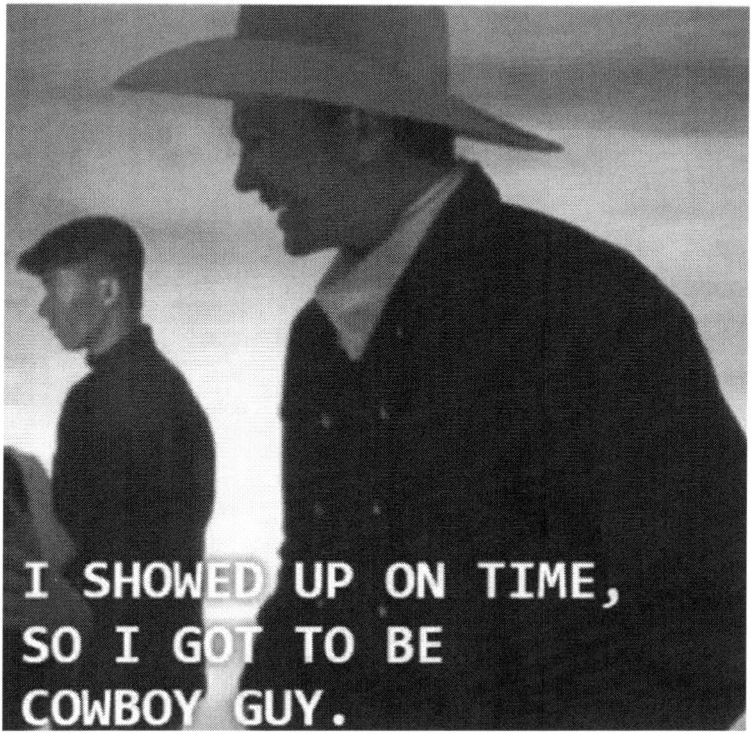
I SHOWED UP ON TIME,
SO I GOT TO BE
COWBOY GUY.

How I feel when the enemy team calls me a hacker while I'm not using hacks

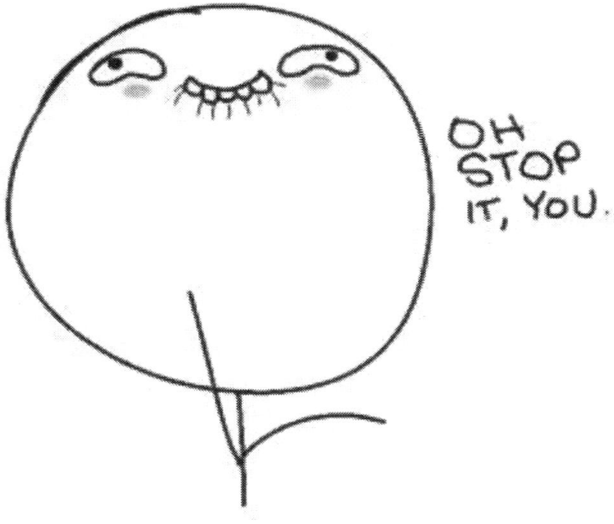
OH STOP IT, YOU.

Me: He killed me completely fair

Also Me: Say it was lag

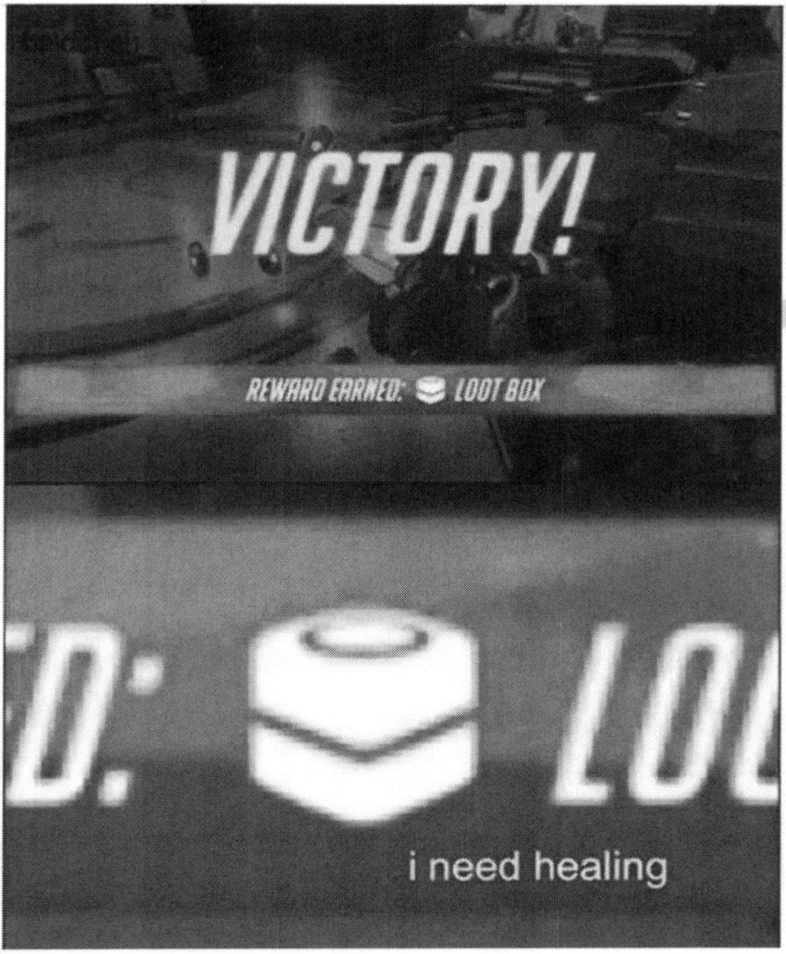
VICTORY!
REWARD EARNED: LOOT BOX
i need healing

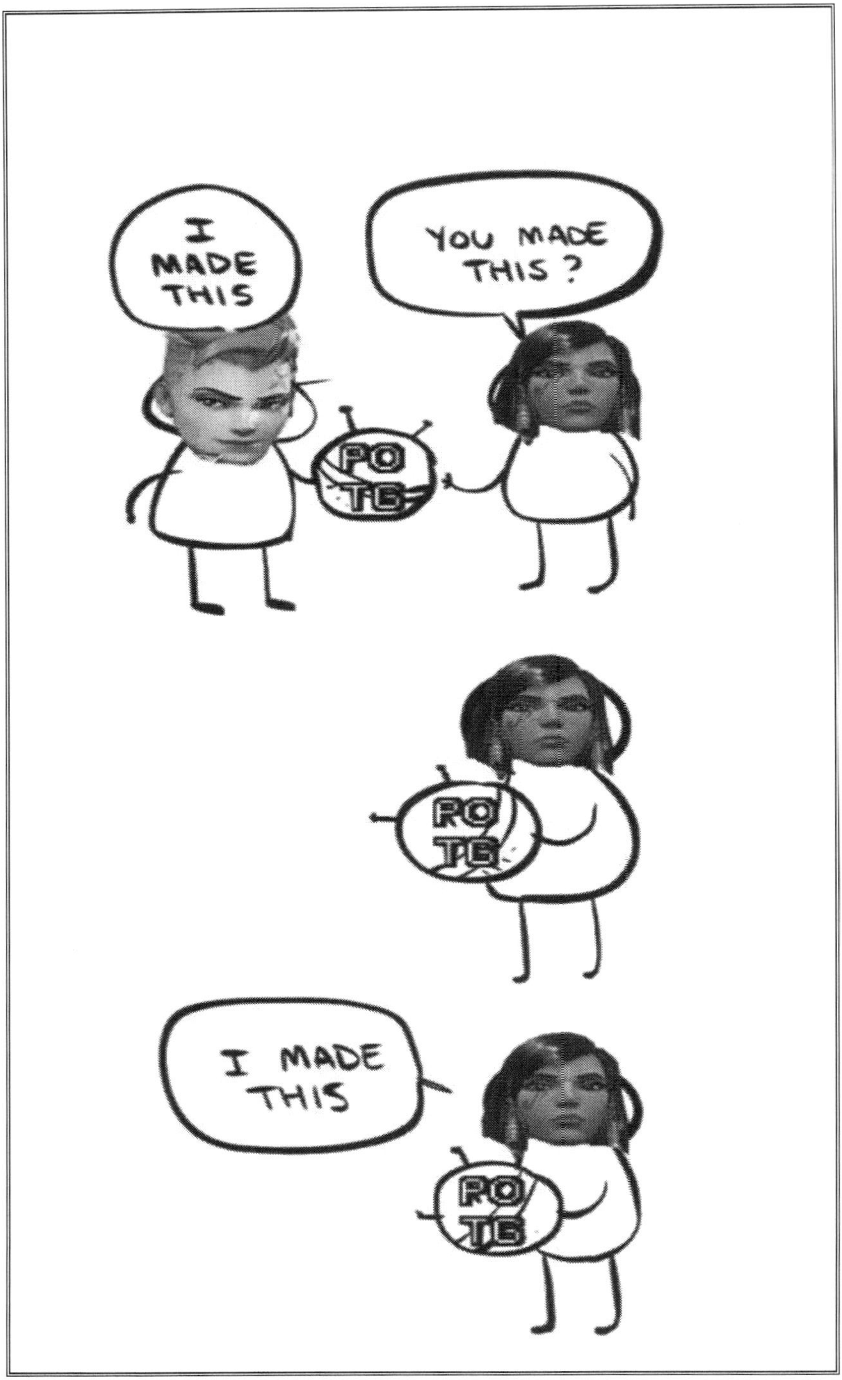
I MADE THIS
YOU MADE THIS?
PO TG
PO TG
I MADE THIS
PO TG

When you're trapped in Zarya's Ult and you hear "FIRE IN THE HOLE!"

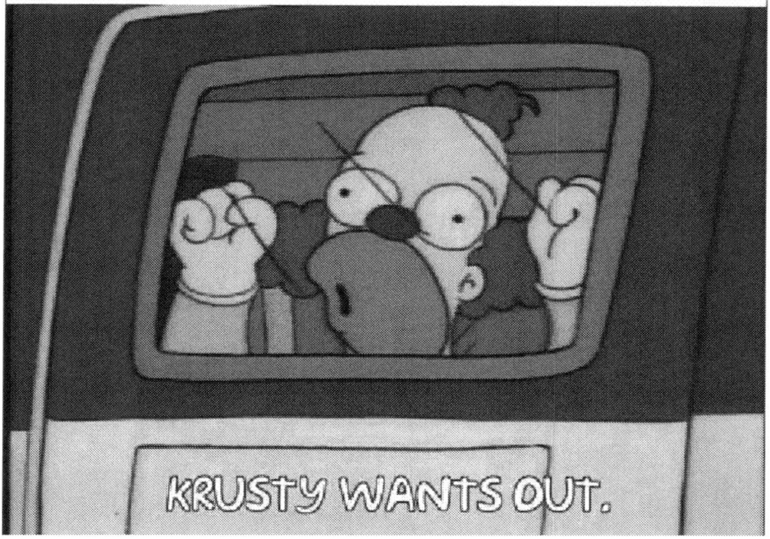
KRUSTY WANTS OUT.

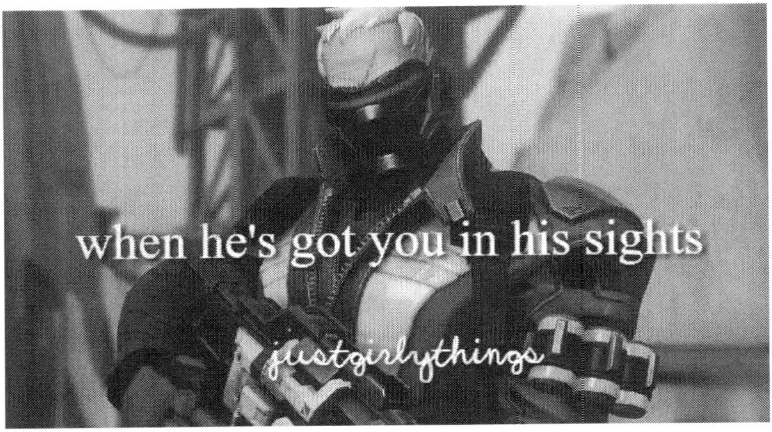
when he's got you in his sights
justgirlythings

mfw I get hit by Reinhardt's ult

The floor is the payload

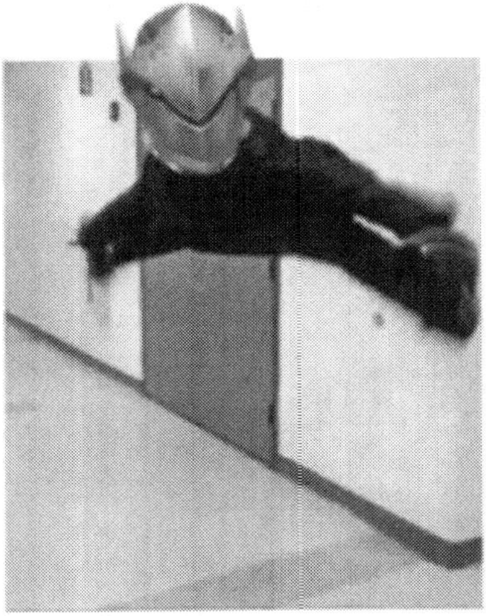

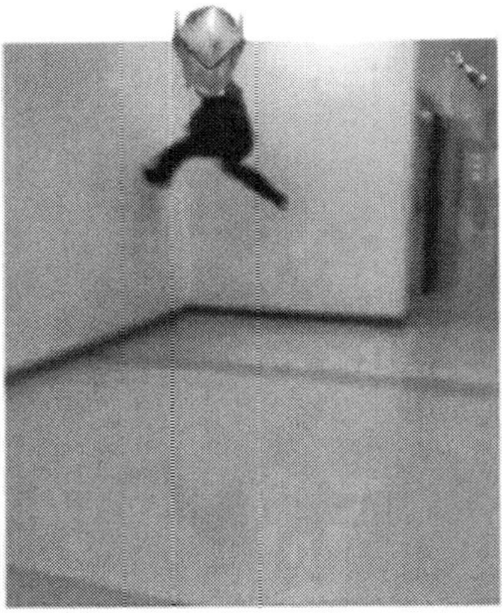

When the Reinhardt you were healing suddenly charges off to god knows where, leaving you with the enemy team:

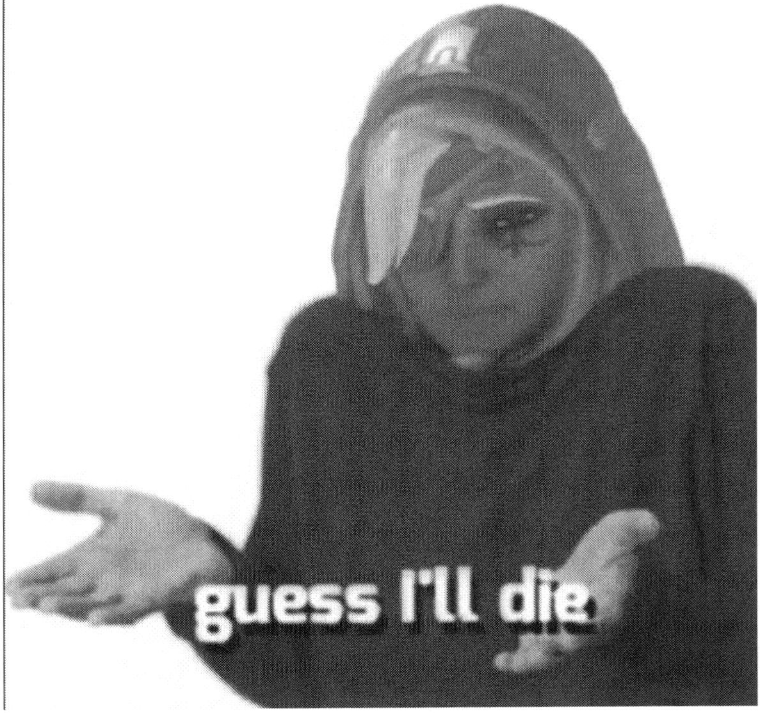
guess I'll die.

Attack Commences in 30
Seconds.jpg

When you manage to survive roadhog's hook

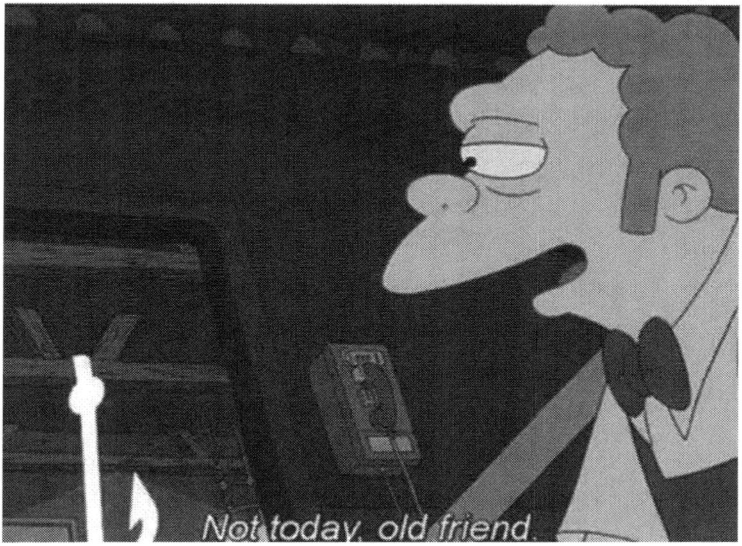
Not today, old friend.

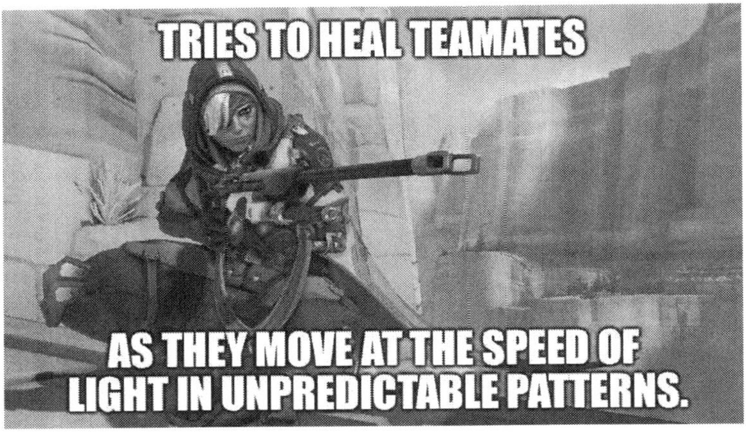
TRIES TO HEAL TEAMATES
AS THEY MOVE AT THE SPEED OF
LIGHT IN UNPREDICTABLE PATTERNS.

When your team is doing horribly so someone leaves and the 6th person that joins is a 9 year old saying "hi guys welcome to my youtube"

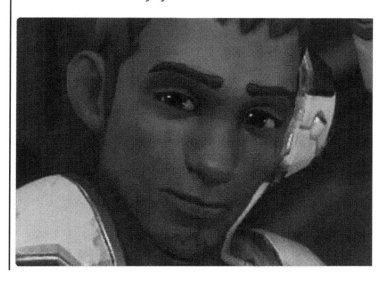

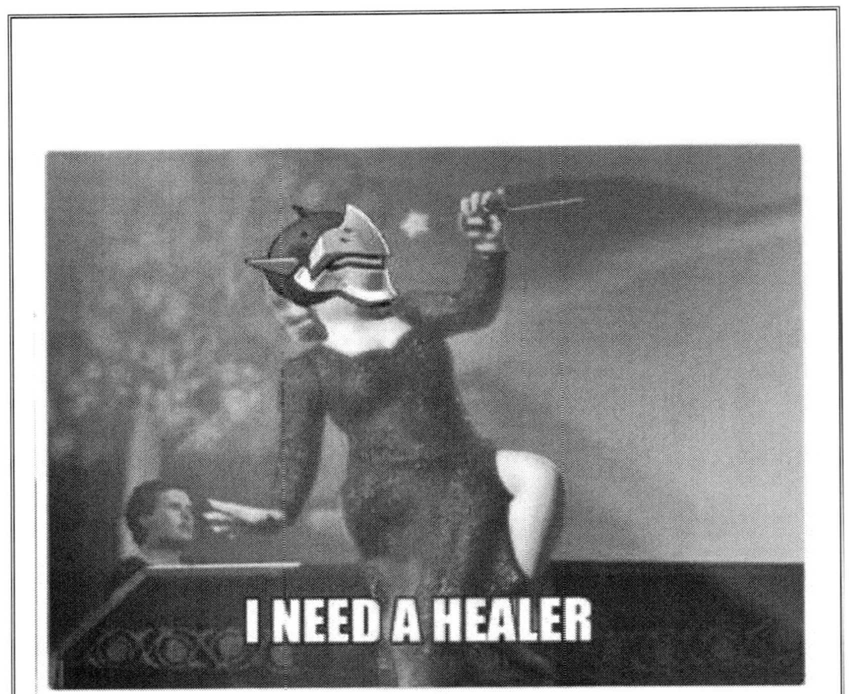
I NEED A HEALER

When someone overextends and begs for healing

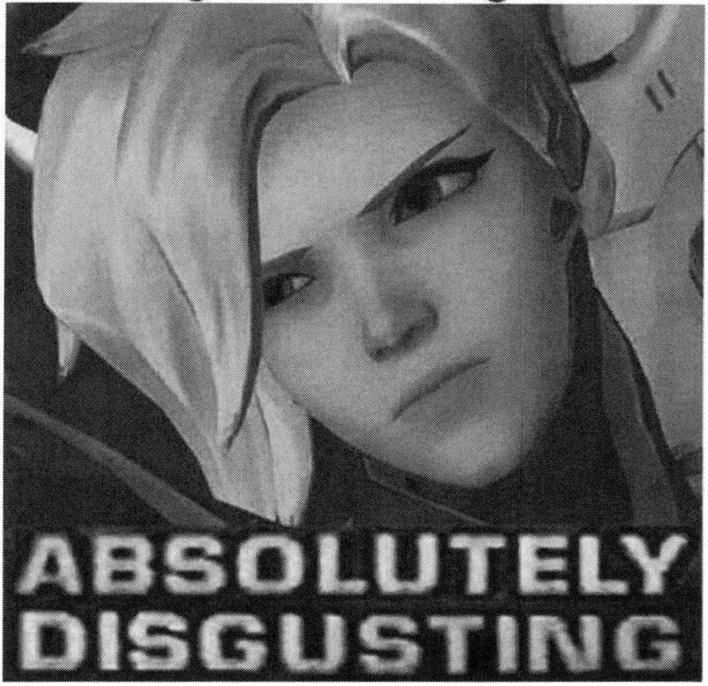
ABSOLUTELY
DISGUSTING

I have basically seen two types of D'va fanart online

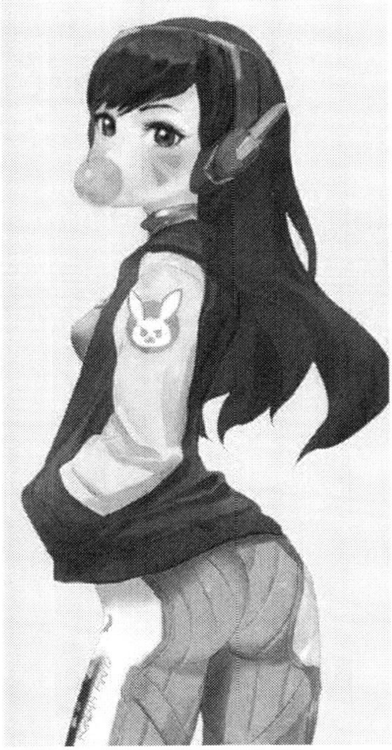

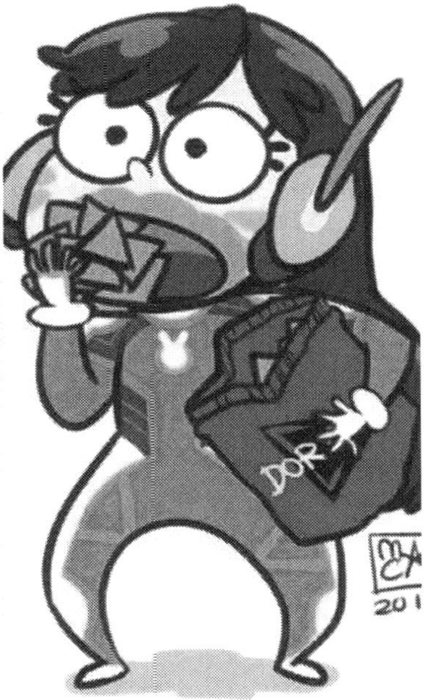
DOR

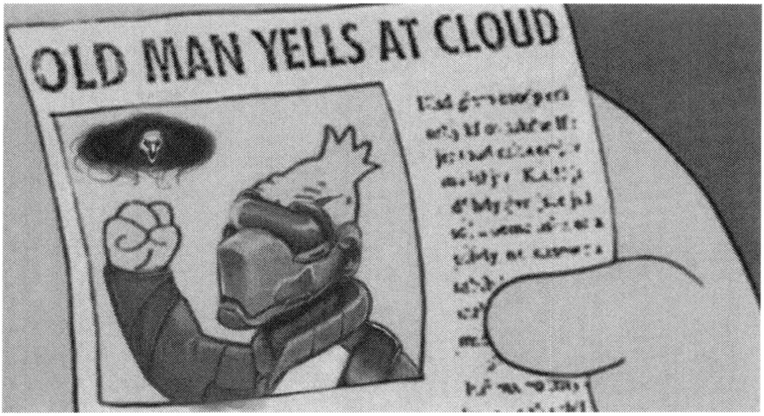
OLD MAN YELLS AT CLOUD

"I main Tracer, I'm too quick for Roadhog to hook me"

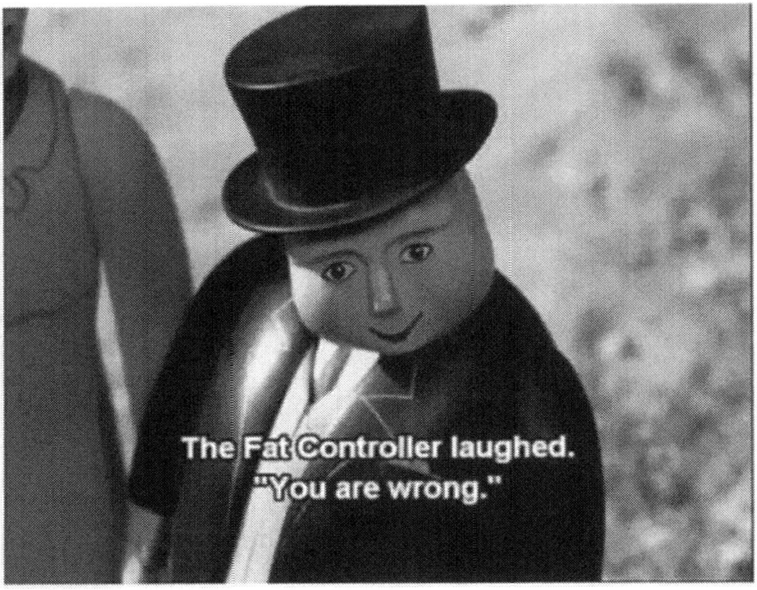
The Fat Controller laughed.
"You are wrong."

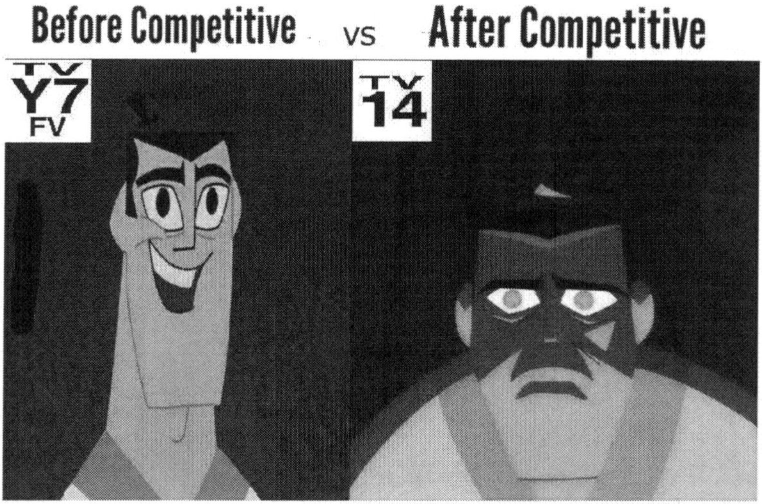
Before Competitive
vs
After Competitive
TV
Y7
FV
TV
14

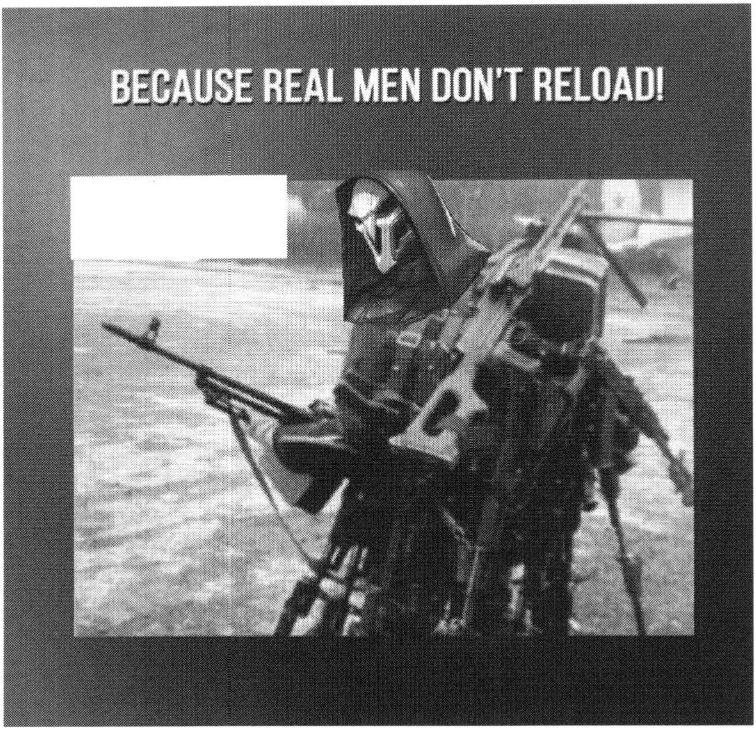
BECAUSE REAL MEN DON'T RELOAD!

you can't lose the objective if you don't play the objective

Mercy: "Now I won't heal you for the rest of the match."

Me:

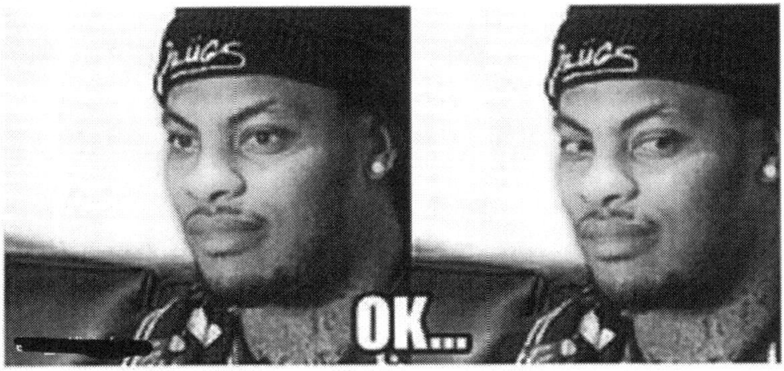
OK...

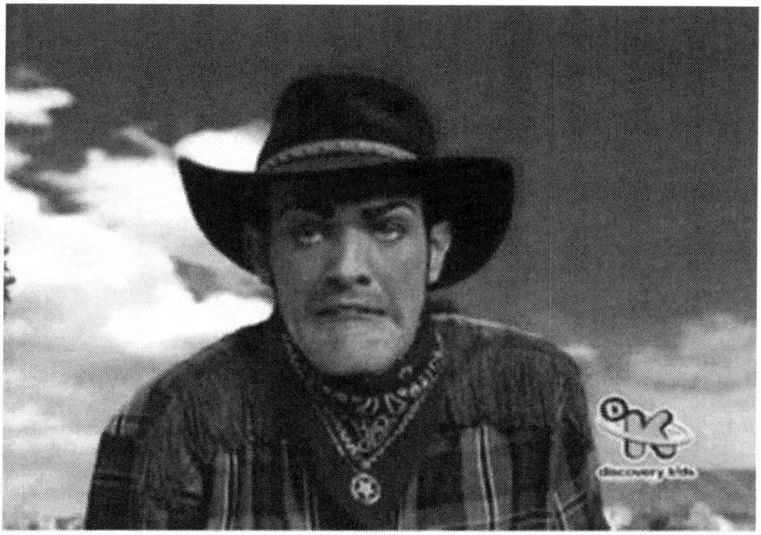
discovery kids

when your McCree Ult doesn't kill anyone

We need a healer!
Patrick, that's Junkrat
Yes

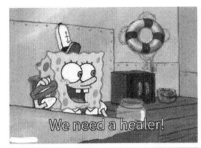

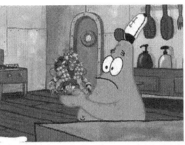

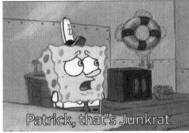

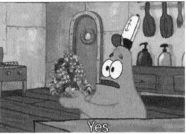

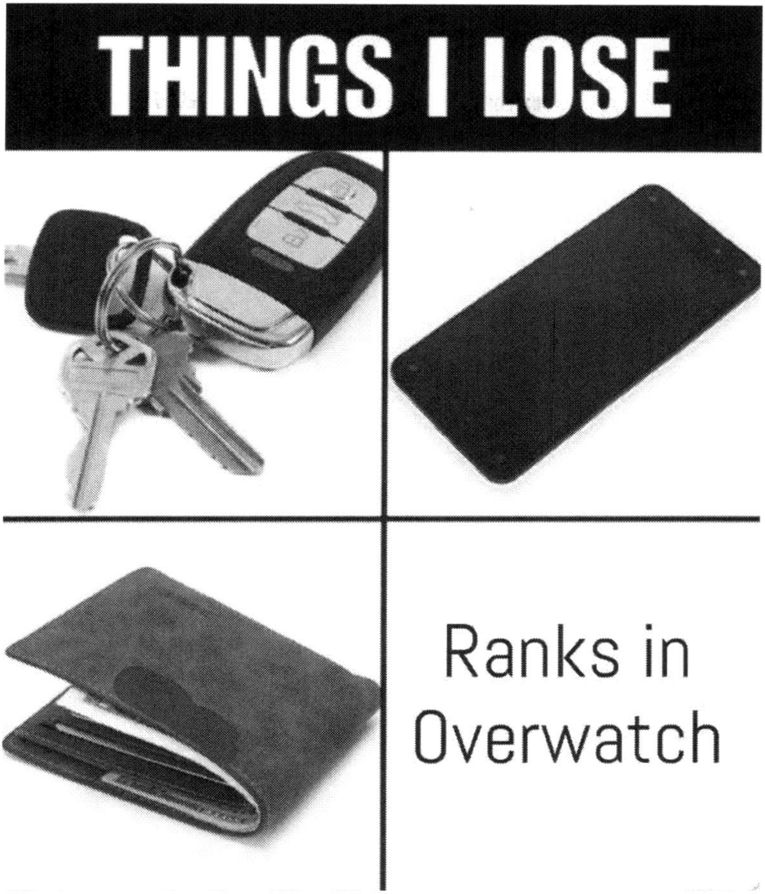
THINGS I LOSE
Ranks in
Overwatch

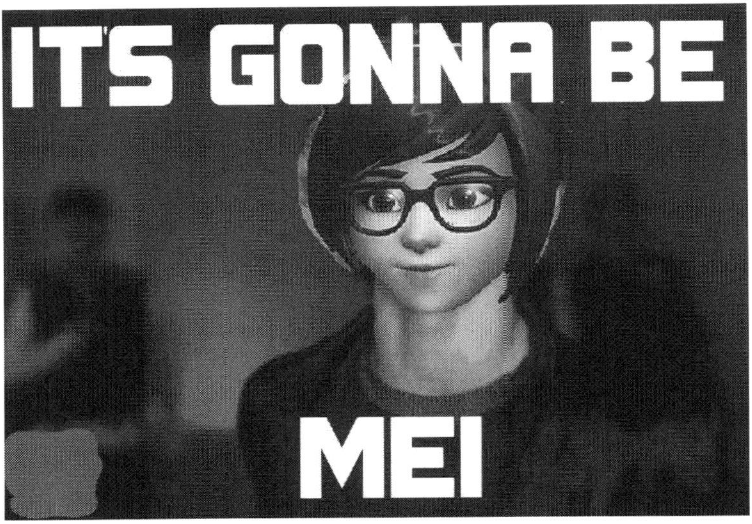
ITS GONNA BE
MEI

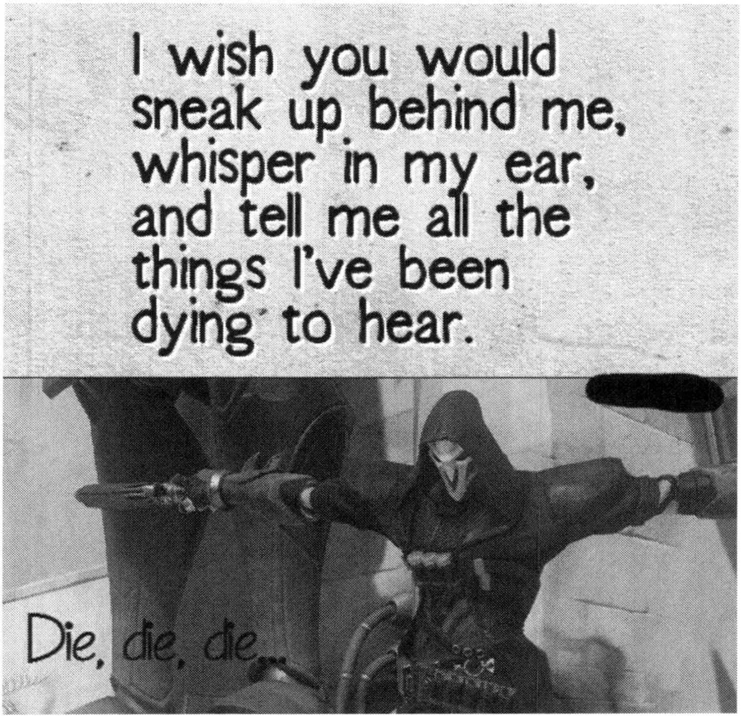
I wish you would sneak up behind me, whisper in my ear, and tell me all the things I've been dying to hear.
Die, die, die...

when they can't just say gg

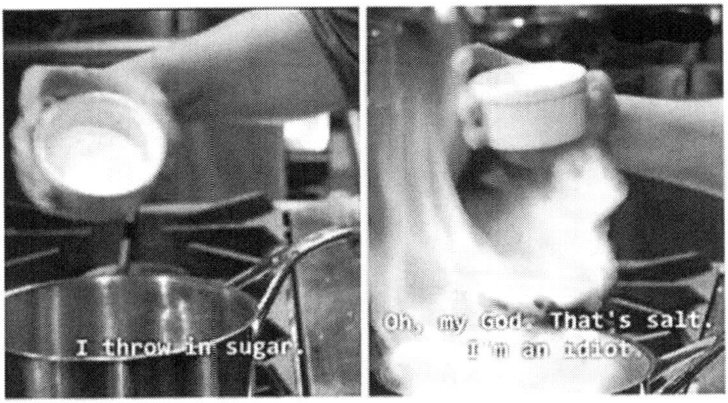
I throw in sugar.
Oh, my God. That's salt.
I'm an idiot.

Level 1 Mercy player vs Level 101 Mercy player

when you can hear footsteps behind you

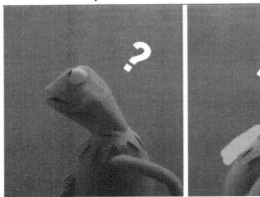

When someone doesn't like your favourite video game:

That's fine, I get that,
but you're wrong and I hate you.

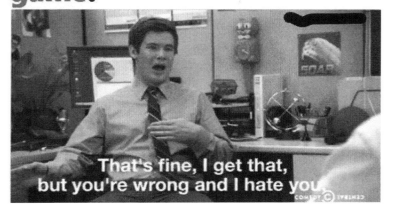

when you lose multiple games in a row and still say "gg"

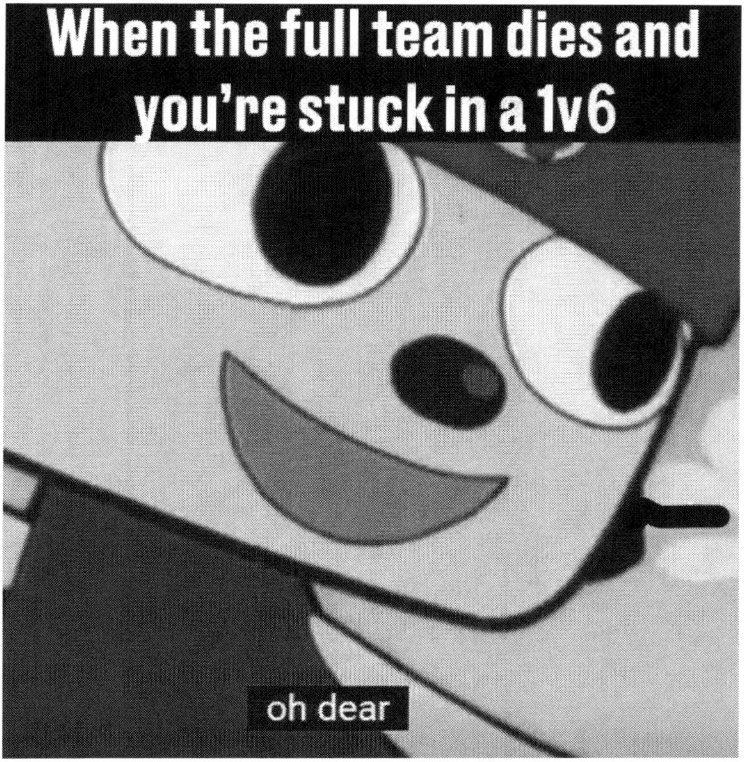
When the full team dies and you're stuck in a 1v6
oh dear

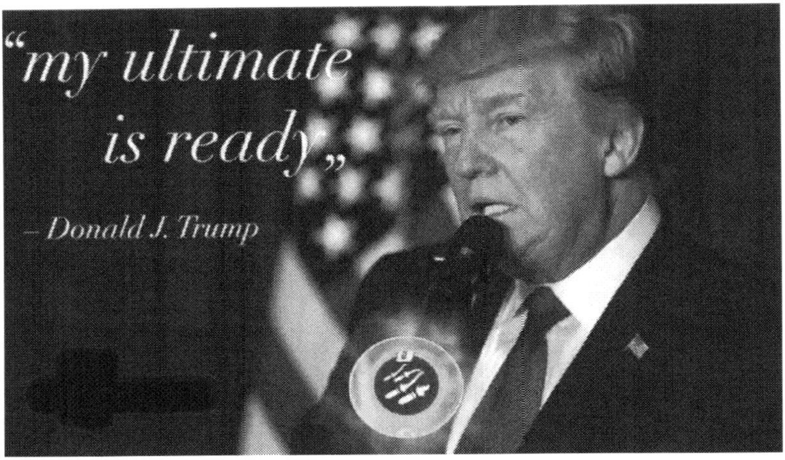
"my ultimate
is ready"
– Donald J. Trump

when you hear "IT'S HIGH NOON"

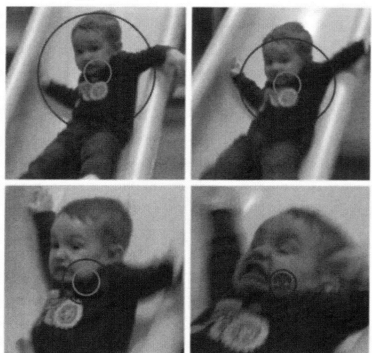

Group Up **Push the Payload** **Trickle in**

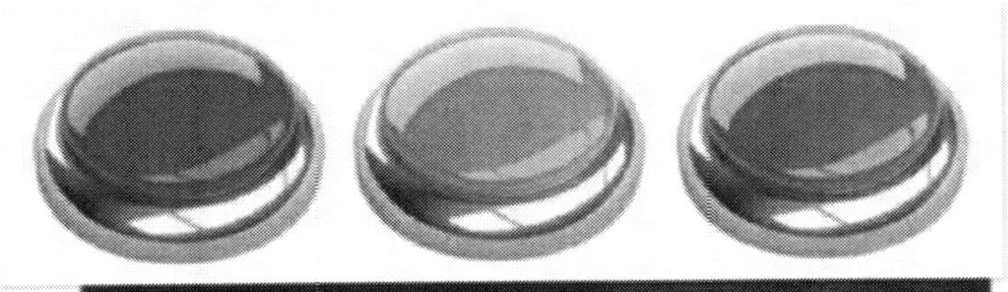

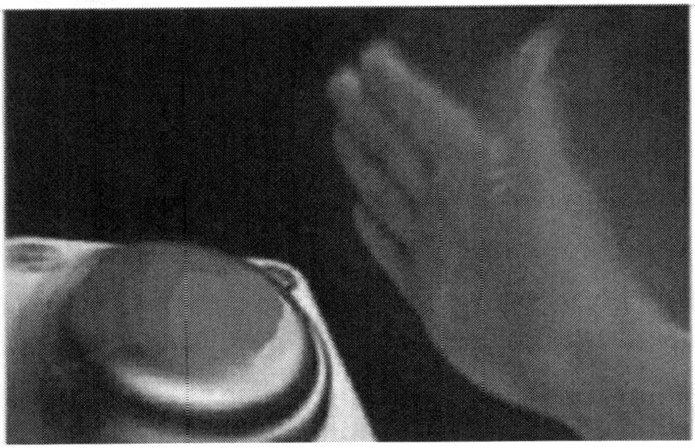

'Contest the point! Where is my team?"
Team:

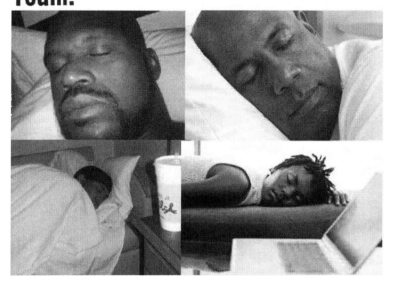

"Soilder 76 isn't a real healer"
Me:

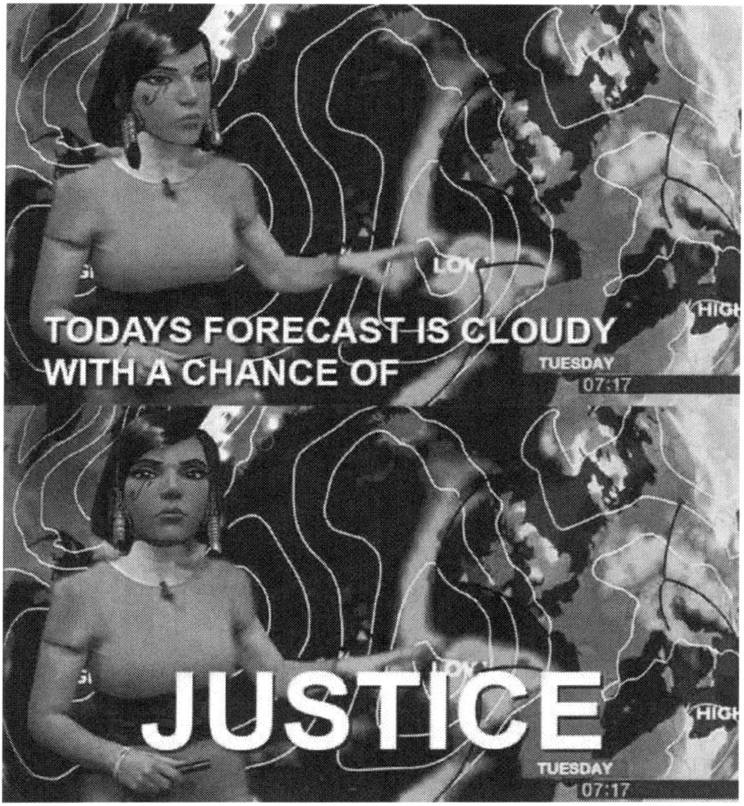
LOW
HIGH
TODAYS FORECAST IS CLOUDY
WITH A CHANCE OF
TUESDAY
07:17
LOW
JUSTICE
HIGH
TUESDAY
07:17

Me: I really shouldn't fly into crossfire to heal our frontline. It's too dangerous.

Me to me: Heroes never die.

When you're about to boop an enemy off a ledge but they only move an inch

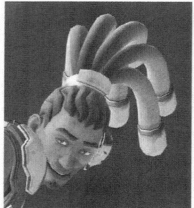 

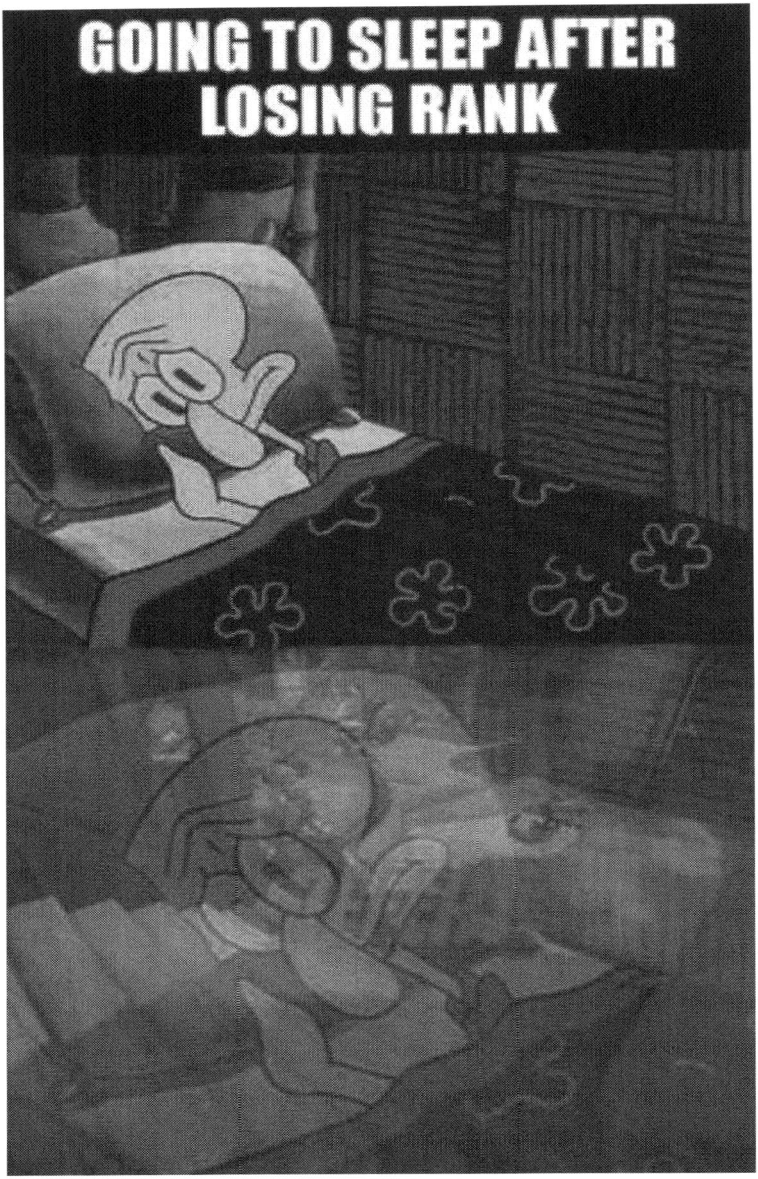
GOING TO SLEEP AFTER LOSING RANK

When your teammates are spamming "I need healing" but you're on healing song and there's nothing else you can do

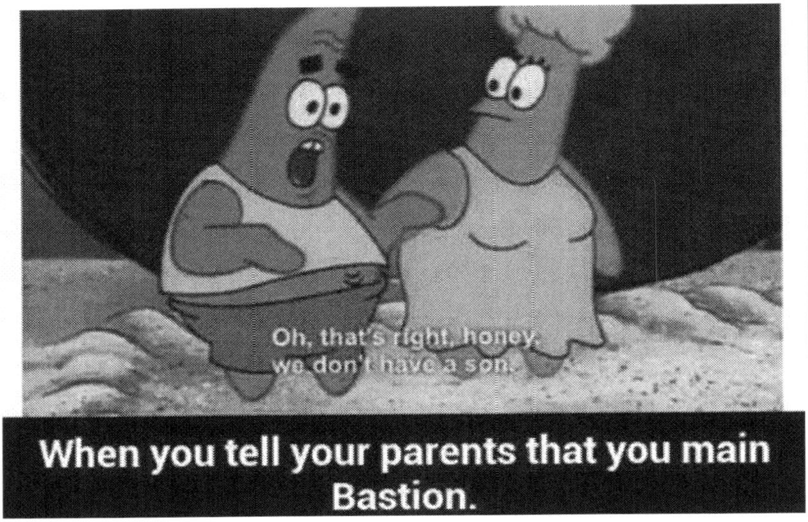
Oh, that's right, honey,
we don't have a son.
When you tell your parents that you main Bastion.

Work together as a team
Rush in alone and die

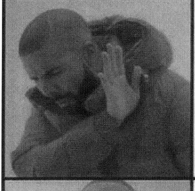

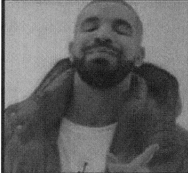

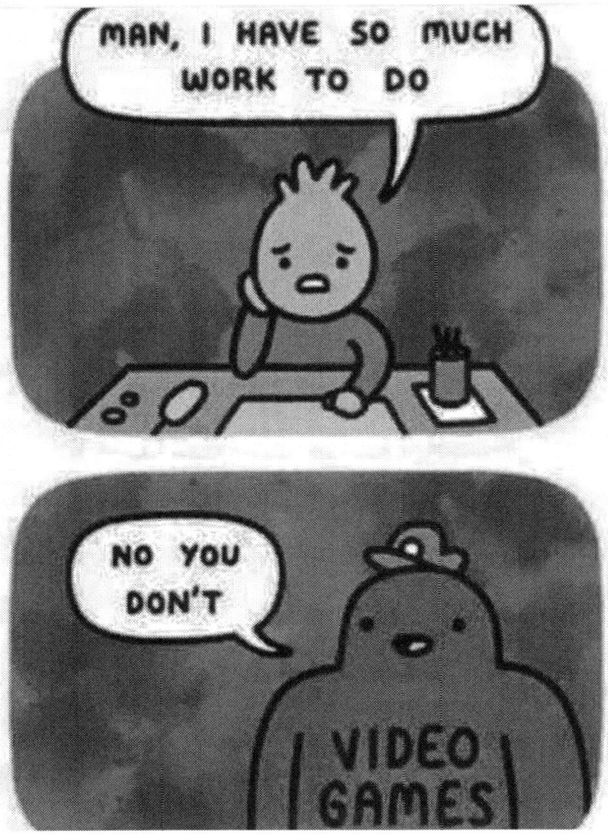
MAN, I HAVE SO MUCH WORK TO DO
NO YOU DON'T
VIDEO GAMES

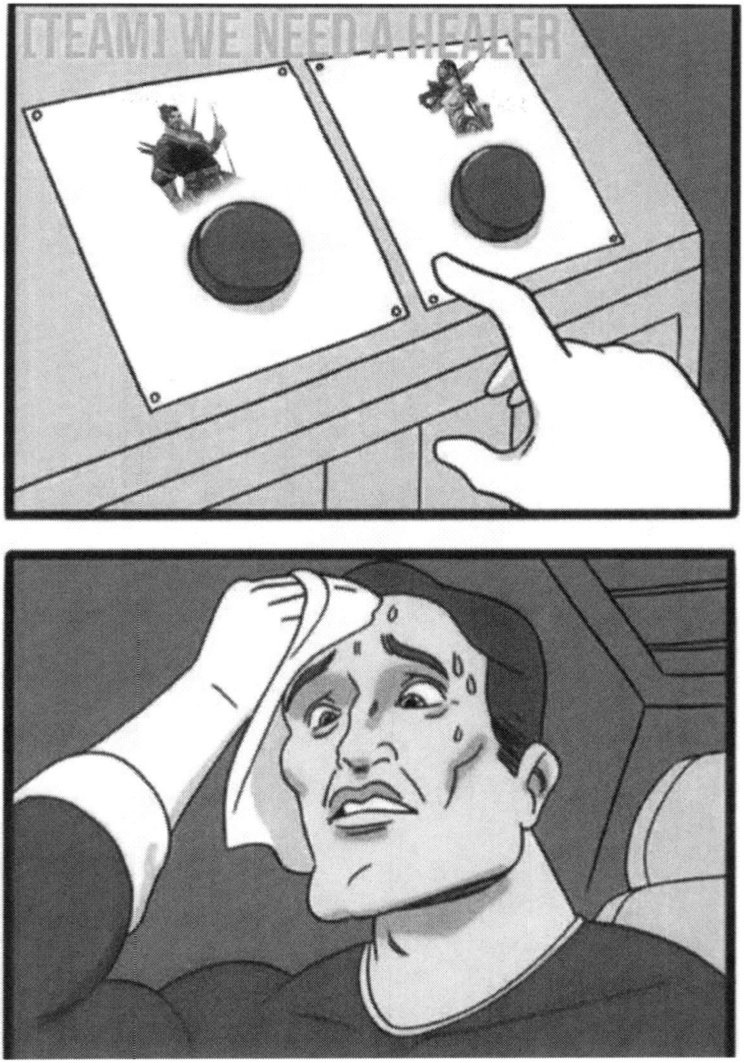
[TEAM] WE NEED A HEALER

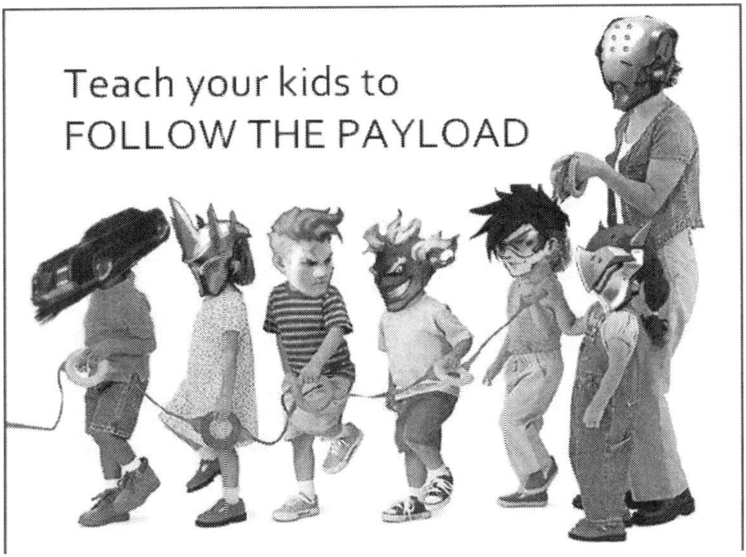
Teach your kids to
FOLLOW THE PAYLOAD

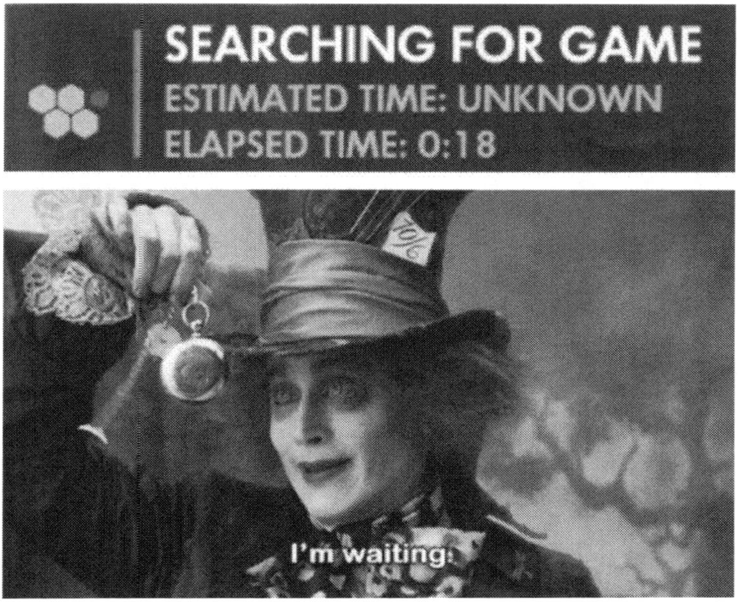
SEARCHING FOR GAME
ESTIMATED TIME: UNKNOWN
ELAPSED TIME: 0:18
I'm waiting.

I HAVE NO IDEA
WHAT I'M DOING,
ELIMINATED
ELIMINATED
ELIMINATED
BUT I KNOW I'M DOING IT
REALLY, REALLY WELL.

25050853R00070

Printed in Great Britain
by Amazon